Autobiography of SAMUEL PLAIN JR.

Copyright © 2017 SAMUEL PLAIN JR.

All rights reserved.

ISBN:
ISBN-13:978-1979043915

DEDICATION
TO THE YOUTH

For the youth before me and many generations to come. Be considerate in your thinking as well as your judgement. Remember life is but a corridor of Windows and Opportunities. One must understand that every thought of the human mind can be Negative or Positive energy. It's the process of Simple mathematics, your thoughts becomes you. So think and judge wisely, and your everyday life will fair opulent results…Remember no matter how brilliant the thought, if its Negative keep it out of your mind…

SENTENCING
APRIL 14, 2000

I had been a fugitive for Eighteen months at this time. I know it sounds crazy right? How could I have been a fugitive, when this was the day I received my Federal Sentence. I was enjoying the view of the Mississippi River, when I heard the US. Marshal rattling chains. It broke my concentration. The holding cell I was in, had a unbelievable view of downtown Memphis and the river. Being Incarcerated made me appreciate the small things in life. Plus, this was the closest I was going to get to freedom for a long time. The US Marshal said with a big smile on his face, "Good afternoon!" It almost seemed like he was trying to brighten my spirit. He instructed me to step out the cell. Then told me to turn around and hold up my left leg. Once he had the shackle on my left ankle, he did the same to my right ankle. He then handcuffed me, ran a chain around my waist, through the shackle, then through the handcuffs. Only to put a pad lock through the chain link. He patted me on the back and wished me good luck. Any time you were being transported somewhere, you would be asked to do this process. Every small step I took was harder than the last. I never could get used to walking in shackles. I was taken to a room in the courthouse to wait. Then the US Marshal reappeared, just to take the shackles off again. As I walked in the courtroom, I looked up at US District Judge Bernice Donald and I noticed she was reading something. Mark A. Mesler was my attorney. Mark motioned me over to the defendant table. I was his very first Federal case. I looked across the table at the US Attorney Tony Arvin. I also looked across this huge courtroom, to see my family in the back. This lifted my spirits tremendously. Then the US Marshal commanded everyone in the courtroom to stand for the Honorable US District Judge Bernice Donald. The Government called its first witness head ATF agent Michael Rolling. His testimony mainly consisted of what Clifford's lying ass had to say. Clifford was the juvenile on my case. Judge Bernice Donald saw right through this bullshit. She appreciated all the agents discovery's but didn't want to hear all the [he say she say]. Mark never cross examined the agent, there was no need to. I told Mark that I didn't want to give a testimony. Two months earlier I had agreed to talk to Agent Michael Rolling about what I did. Clifford lied about us being there with him. The agent asked me who was committing all these assaults? I said "me", I told him everything I did. They reassured me they wouldn't use what I said against me. Judge Bernice Donald is so wise, she didn't want to hear anything that anyone had to say except for me. During my cross examination US Attorney Tony Arvin did his job and asked me one question. What was the plan? The Government knew Corry had nothing to do with this. I said the plan was to shoot the people as they run out the house. That the bomb was only a diversion. My original indictment carried from one to ten years. Corry and I were surprised to find that we had been called to court one morning. Clifford told the Government Corry and I were the ones that bombed the house. The Superseding Indictment was for the bombing of a house. This Indictment carried

Autobiography of Samuel Plain Jr.

up to thirty years no less than ten. Corry and I where facing forty years in prison. I told the [PSI] people in my pre-sentencing Investigation report, that I was taking Corry home that morning. US Judge Bernice Donald had a problem with the way my PSI was written. It was basically a case built off of Clifford Green's testimony, until I agreed to tell the truth about what I did. As Judge Bernice Donald handed down my sentence to me she said "Take this time to think about what you did to get here. Reflect on your action because if you attempt something of this nature again it will be LIFE IN PRISON! Not the six and a half years that you're receiving today!" US Marshal took me out of the courtroom, and shackled me once again with chains. On the ride back to Mason Tennessee to the CCA holding facility I thought about what Judge Bernice Donald told me. I have everyday of my life since. She taught me more than I learned in my whole life. I felt it. I was going to prison. Being mad at Clifford Green, Michael Rolling, Verrod Hampton or US. Attorney Tony Arvin wasn't the answer. They didn't send me to prison. Samuel Plain Jr. did by the choices I made. I created my very own demise for myself. Corry received 3 years and 10 months for hanging out with a old friend. That had become a Menace in Society. I remember thinking to myself how did I get here?

Autobiography of Samuel Plain jr.

The Summer of '96.

The summer started off hot. School was out and girls were everywhere. I had a raggedy ass Cadillac. It was clean though. I had bought a 425 Engine that my cousin Zo and I put in it. My dad had taught us everything there was to know about cars. We washed it up, put a for sale sigh on it, and it was ready to be sold. I pulled up on Barbwood. We were hanging out all night, until the track slowed down. We went in the house to play the super Nintendo game. Now this was my partner Terry's grandma's house. All the junkies would come here to buy their dope and it was a safe place for them to get high. Even my partner mama got high. Her name was Marie. It was her day to day routine to beat people out their money and help Terry sell his dope. She was a natural hustler. She had a boyfriend named June, he was a Vietnam Veteran. He would get so drunk and have war flashbacks making machine gun noises and screaming,"I got you motherfucker!" Then he would stand up and beat on his chest. We would all bust out laughing! Terry's grandmother, Ms. Mabel was like my grandmother, considering she lived one house over from our house on Durby Street. The Airport ended up buying all the houses on Durby Street. We moved to a neighborhood in East Memphis. Coincidently, Ms. Mabel moved to the same neighborhood, just a few blocks away. All the children would call her " Mama. Mabel."

One day, we were in the house playing the Nintendo, when all a sudden we heard a big "BOOM!" Me, Terry, and Lil Yo ran outside to find the Cadillac smashed in. An old woman had fallen asleep at the wheel and wrecked into it. It worked out in my favor because I got more from her insurance than I would have selling it. The next day, I had the car towed, and had an estimate done. They said fixing it would cost more than the car was worth. Bobby Smith, who owned the body shop on Beale Street, wrote up an estimate and I presented it to the old lady. She agreed to pay me $1500, but in payments of $300 a month, for five months.

We left downtown Memphis and went back to East Memphis when I saw this fine Red-Bone walking down the street. She was wearing this big golden necklace with an African medallion. I hopped out the car and approached her like I was interested in getting her number, but really I just wanted her gold necklace.

I said real smooth, "What's up Lil momma? What's your name?"
She replied, with an attitude, "Why?"
I said, with a smile, "Because, you my type.", and walked a little closer. She looked at me crazy and said, "Boy, don't walk up on me!"
That's when I said, "Fuck you bitch!", and went to snatch the gold chain
from her neck.

She had good reflexes because she grabbed my hand, and I ended up with the medallion and only half of the necklace. She was too cute, and it was not my

intentions to hurt her. So, I just took what I had and left. We made it back to the 'hood, and I knew from that day on, it was going to be a long Summer.

About a week or so later, Lil Yo and Lil N had broken into this dude Ray's house. They stole all his clothes, jewelry, and guns. They had nowhere else to go, so, of course they came to my house. It was like I had my own place, both my parents had passed away. They started going through everything they had stolen. They had two gold rings and a big gold rope like Run DMC used to wear. That's when I started scheming. I got the rope and grabbed the 12-gage pistol grip shotgun. Zo had beat me to the 45. It didn't have a clip in it so, I didn't know whether it would shoot anyways. Terry sat back and smiled because he knew we were strapped like Japan. This was Lil Yo's way of insuring his survival. He knew I would ride with him. We got Mr. fields, who was a friend of Mama Mabel, to go to the gun shop and get a clip for the 45, and some 12-gage shells. Turned out, Zo got the better end of the deal because the 45 worked, and the 12-gage pump would only shoot four shells then jam up. It didn't matter though, because all I needed was one shot. So, I had a black and chrome 380, and a 12-gage pump. Zo had the 45 and he also had a 12-gage. I wore the gold rope like it was mine, and fuck who knew it.

We were at the Mall of Memphis and all the females were giving me action because I had this big ass rope on. I copped a few phone numbers, then we left and went back to Barbwood. I saw Marcus.

He said, "Toot, let me wear that rope you wore at the Mall last Saturday."

I told him, "I got someone who wants to buy it."
"How much you wanted for it?"
"900."
"Cool!"

He wanted to buy it.
I told him, "If I let you wear it, then you are responsible for it." He reassured me by saying, "I got you."

How about Marcus wore it out to the Mall and ran into the Ray who it was stolen from. He put his press game down and Marcus bitch ass dropped it off! I heard about this bullshit, so I put the 45 in my pocket, mobbed to Danville Square, and I knocked on the door of the apartment Marcus was in. Marcus came outside, the pistol was visible hanging out my pocket.

I asked him, "What happened to my rope?"
He said, "That dude told me he knew Lil Yo broke into his house." Marcus told him, "This my partner Toot rope."
Ray said, "Bullshit, that's my rope."

I didn't want to hear that shit. I told Marcus that he needed to get my $900 up, or this 45 is gonna togo off.

Autobiography of Samuel Plain Jr.

I knew a war was coming between us and the dude they had stolen form, I just didn't know when. I knew this guy wasn't gonna try me too fast. But they had stolen his woman's shit, the kids shit, and the whole 'hood knew who did it. I sat down with Terry, gave him the business as he fired up a blunt. Terry said, "I told you not to let that weak ass boy, wear that rope!"

We hopped in Terry's Cadillac and rode through the 'hood. He had a black 1980 Fleetwood with limo tint on it. At night you couldn't see in and you couldn't see out. Terry saw his friend Jan-Jan, who he was in love with. She was walking with Dedra and two other girls I didn't recognize. I realized one of them was the girl I robbed earlier in the Summer. I rolled the window up real fast and got a really good look at her. I was trying to avoid her, not knowing if she called the police or not. I still couldn't help thinking how fine and super cute this girl was. I blew the horn and rushed Terry to come on so I could wire him up on what was going on.

After I told him what the business was, we went to the Corner Grocery to get me a plate. I had meatloaf, greens and cornbread, for dessert some banana pudding. I also copped a beer. I needed a fast buzz. Terry greedy ass ate my banana pudding before we picked Zo up on Barbwood. We all mobbed up to my house. We were sitting outside, I was eating my plate, and Terry and Zo were talking shit. A Black Rodeo was bending the block real slow and it caught my attention. My instincts kicked in. I noticed this guy looking out the window trying to start something. I asked him "What your hoe ass looking at?" They sped up. Zo and I bailed in the house. Terry screamed through the door, "They turning around!" Zo grabbed the 45 and rushed back outside. I ran to the back room to get my shotgun. By the time I made into the hallway, I heard what sounded like a 38 "POP! POP! POP!" Then all I heard was the 45 going off! 'BOOM! BOOM! BOOM!' This woke up my oldest sister Melody she ran toward the kitchen window. Before she could make it, I shoved her back. I ran outside to see the Rodeo speeding off. Terry and Zo got the fuck out the way because they knew if this shotgun went off, there was a chance they could get hit. I had no real shot, so I never fired one.

All the gunfire made the neighbors run across the street, giving their eyewitness account of what happened to the police. The police told us to get inside because if one of those 45 shells hit us, our heads would explode. I remember talking to the neighbor Mike. He kept saying it looked like something from a movie. He seemed excited.

Later that day, we were inside talking about the gangster shit that had jumped off earlier. I was demonstrating with the shotgun, and accidentally shot the very tv that my dad would sit and watch all the time. Then, of course, I heard Melody sating, "What the hell y'all doing'?"

I saw Rodney at the fast check about a week later. He told me that his homeboy whose gold rope was stolen wanted to squash the beef. Ray, knew we weren't going. I already put the word out someone was going to get planted. Since all that was about to be behind me, it was time to do something constructive.

The neighbor Mike from across the street offered me a job. He had a friend who was the manager of Olive Garden. Her name was Patrice. She agreed to interview me. I ended up with the job. This job was the longest I had ever kept. I was selling weed on the side, too.

One day, my partner Bow-Legged Luke asked me to ride over to this girl house. I didn't want to get caught slipping so I put my 380 in my side and we mobbed. We pulled up to her house. He got out the car and rang the doorbell. I stayed in the car. I saw this Red bone come out the door, and noticed it was the girl I robbed. I knew it was her because the last time I saw her I got a really good look. She went back in the house. I called Luke over and told him we needed to roll because I robbed her for her necklace earlier. He said, "Ok, gimme a sec.", real calm.

Then, I saw a bunch of dudes looking out the window. I cocked my pistol and watched the door. Finally, Luke came and we pulled off. Luke looked at me and said with a chuckle, "Damn fool!" I replied, very seriously, "Ain't shit funny." He dropped me off at the house.

I didn't have this job a week good and Zo called and told me that Terry had come up to the house to get his 45. Come to find out, Terry was asleep when the children ran inside and woke him up saying his mom was dead in the middle of Barbwood. Los gave Terry a ride to get the 45. Then he took Terry to Austin Wood.

Terry's sister, Felicia, had a baseball bat and was already over at June's momma's house. Felicia was beating June with the bat when she saw Terry was about to shoot him. She tried stopping Terry but couldn't and he shot June twice in the leg and hip. He never walked right since.

Terry jumped back in the car with Los. He took Terry to Orange Mound and dropped him off on Spottswood at Mac's store. He gave Los the pistol and told him he would get up with him. Now the police were looking for Los, his yellow Cadillac, and Terry, high and low. Terry was staying at my house, on the run, and Los turned himself in. Los ended up getting two years for Aggravated Assault. When they found Terry, they gave him six months at STC for Aggravated Assault. Attorney Mark A. Mesler, kept Terry's case in Juvenile court. Terry never saw adult jail.

The Summer was almost over and school had started back. This meant that my birthday was coming up soon. I didn't think it would be too good, but I didn't have to work that day. My 18th birthday turned out perfect! My sister gave me $1000! I dropped the money down on a White on White '86 Cadillac. I was clean as fuck for a 18yr. old. Tupac was killed the month before. His CD hit the town before it was ready because some train robbers had hit the train and stole it. Everybody was bumping The Don Killuminati: The 7 Day Theory.

A couple weeks later. I was at the school house riding when I saw that cute Red-Bone I robbed, but this time we caught eyes. She had on a smaller gold necklace this time. She was rolling her thumb through the necklace, looking at me like she knew exactly who I was. I smashed on pass with my mug on, as she grit me back. I asked Terry's cousin Lakeisha to ask that girl what she had against me. The next day Keisha, told me that I had robbed her for her Herring Bone. I just smiled and told her she had me mixed up. Keisha also told me her name, Reagan. And now I know she hadn't called the police.

Later that week I bumped into Skeet, June's nephew. He told me that he was gonna blow Terry's ass off when he gets out. Thats when i said. "We can get to shooting." He

hurried up and said, "My beef is not with you, Toot." I told him "If you got beef with Terry, then you got beef with me." It was cold outside. I hopped back in the car and as I'm pulling back up the street, I saw Deidra and Reagan. I jumped out the car fresh to death. Green and White Polo sweater with the Polo Khakis and the Icy White Reeboks, smelling just like Fahrenheit.

I said, "Reagan, let me get two minutes of your time." This time she was all smiles. I asked her "What you got against me?"

She replied "You know you robbed me."

I said, "No I didn't you got me mixed up with someone else, so you mean to tell me the police looking for me?"

She said "No, I ain't no police bitch!"

I told her," That don't make since. If someone pulled a gun on you, why didn't you call the police?"

That's when she said really quick, "Boy, you know what you did, quit playing with me!"

I said, "Since your convinced I did this, give me a chance to make it up to

you." She said, "How you gonna do that?"

I told her to let me call her and we could talk about it. So,

she gave me her
number. I said bye to them and jumped in the car, thinking to myself, Damn she was cute! Then I hit the block again and rolled back up on them and asked if they needed a ride and where they were going. Of course, Reagan replied, "Don't push your luck." I swatted off.

The next day Zo and me were at the schoolhouse fucking with some girls. When some guys from Walter Simmons started hating on me. They were in a raggedy ass Box Chevy, and they started hitting me up with gang signs, representing their projects, and throwing up Deuce. They started calling me and Zo "bitch ass boy" and " hoe ass boy." They were just mad because I was clean as fuck in my Cadillac and I had all the girls fucking with me. I jumped out of traffic and went to the house. I was 38 hot! I went inside and Melody was on the couch watching All My Children and my gage was under couch so I couldn't get to it. I went back outside and asked Zo where his gage was at He told me, "In the closet." So, I went and got it. Zo and me mobbed back up to the school. By this time, the girls had made it further up the street. We passed the school and rode down the street. Low and behold here comes that Box Chevy. So, Zo kept saying, "Give me the gage! Give me the gage!" He was hanging out the sunroof. I ignored him as I pumped a round into the chamber. As soon as the Box Chevy got beside us, I let them have it. "BOOM! BOOM! BOOM!" You would have thought I was holding a fire breathing dragon. Everybody got down on the ground, kids were running and hiding behind anything in sight. The Chevy wrecked into a pole. I pumped three more rounds into it "BOOM! BOOM! BOOM!" Traffic parted like the Red Sea. We shot up the street. I told Zo to put some pimping in, so I could calm down, and take that Rap shit out. Pimping' is old
school R&B. It's mellow feel clams the spirit.

I stopped by my Auntie Harriet house, and put the Pump under her garage. Then we cruised to Third World and hung out on Durby Circle at my Auntie Pam's house for the rest of the day.

While over at her house, she started to talk to me and Zo. She asked what did we do, because we had been over there all day. Zo and I answered at the same time "Nothing!" She proceeded to tell us that my cousin Bryan had killed somebody. The police kicked in his mom's Cheryl door. My auntie Pam and Cheryl are my mother's sisters, so I was close to my cousins. I asked her "Bryan or Ryan?" They were twins. She said "I'm not sure which one boy! But I know y'all did something, there better not be any police over here looking for y'all!"

I guess she thought she was psychic. Hell, she might be. She always seemed to know these things.

Zo and I turned on the NEWS, we saw it was Bryan who shot a man in the chest. The details were sketchy but it was most definitely Bryan. So, Zo and me creeped back to my house late that night. I was on the phone with Reagan when I got a beep. I told her to hold on and clicked over. It was Bryan. He said he needed my help. I asked, "Where are you?" He told me, "Orange Mound." So, I rode back over there and picked him up. He hopped in the car, I said "What's up, cuz?" He said, "I'm fucked up dawg." I creeped out of Orange Mound trying not to attract any attention. I did not want any problem from the Law.

We made it to the house safe and sound and he proceeded to run down the events of the murder. Bryan had just got out of the Penal Farm about two months ago for a probation violation. He told me how he was boosting with this punk who was known for stealing clothes. Bryan said the punk tried locking him in a house and asked to suck his dick. That's when he shot him twice in the chest at close range with a 38. I thought to myself, This story sounded kinda sketchy. The punk was known for getting money, so I think Bryan tried to rob him and the robbery went wrong. After he shot him, he grabbed the keys and started unlocking the door, but he had blood on his hands and ended up leaving bloody fingerprints behind. When he got out the house, he stole the punk's '93 Maxima, and drove over to his girlfriend's house in Kansas Court. He left the car in an ally not too far from her house.

When he went back to burn the car, the police had already found it. He was all over the NEWS because he left his fingerprints everywhere. He was no doubt their number one suspect. The next day, Zo and I went to my cousin Randy's house. Randy had a girlfriend named Bianca that was a nurse. They had no children. We were all drinking trying to ease Bryan's mind of his problems. I noticed there was blood on Bryan's patent-leather Reeboks. That's when it hit me, I knew Bryan was going to prison. I told him he needed to throw those shoes away. I used Bianca's phone to call Reagan to try to get my mind off all that was going on around me. She was real short. Deidra was over at her house, so, she wasn't trying to rap at that moment.

Randy was feeling too good and Bianca was tired of us being over at her house. I was supposed to be at work by this time, but I had a buzz and said, "Fuck it."

We ended up driving to Scutterfield over to Randy's baby's momma's house. Her name was Nita. As Bryan and me were talking, Channel 3 NEWS came on the television. They still weren't releasing much information, just blasting Bryan's picture and name all over the NEWS. I told Randy we needed to go. He was so drunk. This was like Mission Impossible. We finally left, dropped Randy off, and made it back to the house. The next couple days I noticed Bryan started getting real careless. The police had canvased the neighborhood where he left the car and while talking to witnesses they stumbled upon his girlfriend. We didn't know what she was telling the police but Bryan kept allowing her to call the house. I started getting nervous. Then he did the unthinkable and invited her over to the house! Zo and I left and went to Durby Circle the next day. As soon as we pulled, up my

Autobiography of Samuel Plain jr.

Auntie Pam was standing in the doorway. She told us to come over there because she needed to talk to us. She told us that she knew we were over at Randy's house drinking and we had Bryan with us. She went on to tell us that we needed to get away from around him because she dreamt we had all been locked up.

Shortly after, the police kicked Cheryl's door in again looking for Bryan. Bryan kept calling Pam's house all day, and she kept telling him we weren't there. We were outside hooping when a strange car pulled up. Bryan jumped out. I walked over to him and it seemed he knew I was through fucking with him on this matter. That he was on his own now. I told him I loved him but he brought his female to the house, and she had been talking to the police. He gave me a look of understanding and I hugged him. A week later the police finally caught him.

Within that week of his capture, my other cousin called home from the Penal Farm. He was serving a four-year sentence for a carjacking. He said he heard about what happened at the school house, and he had also heard about Bryan. He went on telling me I needed to sit my ass down somewhere before I catch a murder charge. That could have easily been me instead of Bryan.

Ms. Mabel, Keisha and I went to see Terry at STC. I had a lot to tell him. Only thing was, his counselor was supervising the whole visit. It felt good to see my friend even though the visit only lasted 30 minutes. I didn't get a chance to finish telling him about what happened at the school house. He put his finger over his lips as if to let me know it wasn't safe to talk in here.

I dropped Ms. Mabel off on Barbwood. Zo and I picked up Reagan and Deidra. Reagan had this Keith Sweat album that she would play all the time. Zo and Deidra were just fucking partners, just having fun. They were nothing like Reagan and I. We were in a relationship. Reagan wanted a baby and I was trying to give her one.

New Year's Eve night, Reagan and Deidra were

babysitting Shay's baby. I picked them up about 9:00. Reagan wanted to shoot my gun. She kept asking me. I finally agreed to let her. The clock said 12:00 am. Zo and I were in the front yard. Zo let his gage rip and I came right behind him. That's when I saw the police

across the street at the school. They kept driving to the back of the school. Little did I know, they thought we were shooting at them.

They were calling for back up while we were in the house reloading. Reagan met me at the door saying, "Toot, let me see it." As I was walking through the kitchen, I saw the police office in a crouching position through the kitchen window. I said, "Reagan. Police! As soon as I said that, she turned with the gun pointed right at the police officer. He screamed, "Put the gun down!" When she realized the police were at the door, she screamed and dropped the shotgun on the floor. The officer grabbed the gun off the floor. The police made everyone in the house walk out backward with our hands high in the air. Lil Yo didn't want to come out the house. The police had to go in and clear the house. Yo was really bullshitting. I was hoping they let us go. They had us on the wall stretched out with our hands up. Lil Yo finally come out the house. After the police saw that the house was clear, they calmed down. The only thing saved us was the man that stayed next door. He came outside shooting his 38, while the police had us against the wall. They all started to pull their gun out getting down moving towards the shots. My neighbor went back inside. The police knocked on his door but he didn't answer. I said, "See! Everyone shoot their guns on New Year's! They let us go, but confiscated my gun. They actually thought we were shooting at them. I knew then that this was going to be a crazy year.

I bought a '78 Blue Cadillac Sedan Deville parked it in the backyard. There was nothing happening on Barbwood. The track had dried up. I started back posting up every day and got it back rolling. Terry had a month left before he got out. I had everything running smooth. No bullshit, period. Things were going good for me.

Reagan was throwing up like crazy. I had made a baby. It was a must that I get some money. Reagan told her mama she was pregnant. They both started crying. Reagan's mama called her daddy on the phone. Her daddy jumped right on the phone talking shit saying, "I don't know who was on top of who, but you getting put on Child Support because I'm on child support." I just gave Reagan the phone so she could talk back to her dad. I walked outside, jumped in my car, and left. I needed something to take my mind off Reagan being pregnant. I pulled up on Barbwood and backed in. Junkies would knock on my window all night. I was posted trying to get it up. This became my daily routine.

Terry was released from STC in February. I gave him the Blue Cadillac. It needed a windshield in the front of it. It ran extremely well I only paid $400 for it. He jumped straight out getting money. I had the track rolling. I told Terry about Reagan being pregnant. He couldn't believe it. I was over Reagan house eating dinner when Terry called me and asked me what should he do about Black.

I asked, "What you mean?"
He said, "He shot up the house!"
I asked, "Shot up who house?
Terry said, "Ms. Mabel's house!" He continued, "That weak ass boy saw

me I guess as soon as I walked up the driveway in the house he started shooting."

I asked, "With kids in the house?!" Terry said, "Yeah!" I said, "I'll be down there."

I pulled up and saw Terry talking to his grandmother. She said, "Y'all don't do anything. I'll handle it tomorrow, a black bastard. I'll fix him." I couldn't believe that this guy actually shot in the house with kids in it. None of the bullets were higher than 4 feet. All head shots for these children. Ms. Mabel filed charges on Black for that. Black was June's brother and he was still upset about his bother getting shot. Now that Terry was out, he wanted revenge. Black ended up being on the run after that.

Terry didn't have a Driver's License but that never stopped him from driving everywhere. One night, the police jumped behind him. He hit the gas on Chuck and him and Bow-legged Luke jumped out in Sunnyfield Cove. Terry jumped in a ditch and swam through a tunnel that came out in Creek Side Apartments. The police thought he was dead because it had been raining and the water levels were up. Bow-legged Luke went to jail. He said he was "to fresh to be getting wet."

Terry wasn't out 30 days good and had me going to get this car off of Flicker Street. Once a car got impounded in Memphis, the only way it could leave the lot was the owner of the car had to buy a tag and register it. So now the blue Cadillac have a tag on the back of it. But his car was registered in my name because he didn't have a Driver's License. After he got his car back, he stayed out of his car. He parked it in the back yard. He knew the car had a hard tag on it that came back to me. I told Zo to leave that car parked, because if the police saw it, they were going to be looking for whoever was driving it that night. Of course, he didn't pay me attention and drove this hot as car anyway. As soon as the police spotted it, they turned the lights on and started to chase it again. Zo drove it to Barbwood, jumped out, and ran this time. The police made sure that whoever was jumping out on them would get caught. They called for back-up and a helicopter. They block off all the streets headed towards Knight Road. Police radios were going crazy... He just ran past me. He's going back south. He's headed Northeast. Now, he's headed Southwest. They didn't catch Zo, so, they came in the house and pulled me out.

"Whose car is this?", they asked.

"It's not mine.", I said.

"I knew you were going to lie to me. Why is the car in your name if
you're not the owner? Are you the one that jumped in

that ditch the other night? No, that's not you. That stupid son-of-a-bitch probably dead. Who did you let drive your car tonight?"

I answered, "I don't know who was driving it."
"Who at your house", they asked. It seemed like the questions would never end. I said, "No one. Just my sister Melody."
He said, "So no one is up nope. I just left."

They handcuffed me and put me in the car and took me home. As I rode up the street, I could see the street blocked off. I could see where the helicopter was concentrating its attention by the house. I was hoping this fool didn't run up there. We pulled up to the house, they knocked on the door, and four police officers went in the house. They came out empty-handed. Zo wasn't in there. He really fucked the police up that night. He ran to Reagan's house and got someone to come get him the next morning.

They let me go, once they didn't fine no one in the house. They wanted to take me to jail but they know I wasn't driving because my white car was parked in the drive way already. They still searched my car even though I wasn't driving it. I knew from the way these guys acted, this shit was far from over.

I stayed in the house like a week I didn't even go over to Reagan's house. I was trying to let shit cool down some. Keisha, Richelle, and Zo walked up to the house. Richelle was all over me until she told me that she couldn't wait to tell Reagan that we had fucked.

I asked her, "Why would you try to intentionally hurt her?" She instantly got an attitude. "Take me home.", she said. I said, "I didn't bring you here."

See. no matter how much of an asshole I tried to be, I was still a gentleman. "Come on.", I said. "I'll take you home."

Zo and Lakeisha wanted to go on Barbwood.
I said, "I'm not going down there. I'm dropping Richelle off on Dungreen

and coming back to the house."
Zo said, "Mane we cool. Come on Toot, we going to be straight,
watch.
I should have stayed in the house. I was cool taking Richelle home. If I just would stuck to the plan...

I turned left on Chuck and saw the police coming off Austin Wood. As soon as they saw my White Cadillac, they hit the lights. I busted a left on Barbwood, hit the gas, and turned in to Ms. Mabel's driveway. I through the car in park and walked in the house. The police sat outside the house waiting on back-up. Then, they came inside.

I stood up and said, "Wassup?"
The officer said, "Put your hands behind your back." I said, "For what?!"
"Evading arrest.", he answered.

They grabbed Lakeisha and Zo, too. ZO was drunk and had a Warrant for his arrest. What happened next, I never saw coming.
The black-haired police said, "You, asshole! You ran from us a couple of weeks back." Zo was so drunk; he was stumbling. The police officer pushed him in the back down the driveway all the while he was handcuffed. Zo stumbled all the way down the hill. He hit the police car face first. It looked like someone had poured red Kool-Aid all over the police car. Blood was everywhere.

Years later this head trauma caused him to have Parkinson's Disease. They took me to 201 Poplar for a steak knife and a blunt. They wrote up the report saying I had
a deadly weapon. I later plead guilty to the charges. I received fines and court cost. Zo went to the hospital for his injuries. I stayed in jail for 16 hours. This shit was nothing like Juvenile Court. Lower level was a dungeon beneath the Earth. You couldn't tell the time of day it was. The cell doors had real bars on it. I didn't eat anything the whole time I was there. On my way out, I

saw Zo coming in. His face was full of blood. They had stitched his head up with over a hundred stitches. I felt bad because he had a Warrant so that meant he had to stay in the dungeon longer. Zo got caught with 23 rocks, when he was a juvenile. He was 17 years old at the time. But the State didn't do anything with the charge until he turned 18. So, he thought the charges just went away. I caught a Cold while I was in there. But I learned a valuable lesson, always have bond money. As soon as I got out, I was back to selling weed. They had pulled my car and I had to get it out the impound. The lot attendant went and got my car from the Impound lot. Only thing, they wanted a repo fee, plus taxes, and tags. I didn't want my car back that bad. At first I did, until they came with all the fees involved.

Zo stayed in jail for two weeks. The court decide to give him probation. Two years worth.

Summer of '97.

My life had started changing in so many ways. Raegan and I found out we were having a little girl, and I knew it was time to start making some serious money. No more just getting by. I was about to be a father to a precious little girl and she had to have the best.

I stayed down and dirty, buying the baby everything she needed before she made her grand entrance into the world. I was getting like two juices, now. I was sitting in the driveway on Barbwood when Chris approached my car. Chris was a junkie. If you have ever seen the movie Friday, he acts just like Ezell. That was actually his nickname. Bodeen, another junkie, stopped him in his tracks. You see, Bodeen kept all the junkies in line for me; he was a knock-out artist. If I were the president, then Bodeen, would be a one-man secret service. He would wait for my "ok" before letting anyone up on me. The shit was funny because he really took his job seriously. Then, there was Terrell, he always stuttered when he talked. He could never get a full sentence out without stumbling over his words. Sam was Ms. Mabel's neighbor.

All the junkies called him "20 strong" because if you didn't have $20 he wouldn't serve you. Sam was a big Man. And not just any type of big; he was muscular, probably because he spent over half his life in the penitentiary. Lil Gary stayed across the street from Ms.

Mabel with his little brother Cliff. Lil Gary stayed locked up all the time. All his Father and uncle did was drink corn liquor.

Up the street stayed, Moe, Lenny, and Phil. Lil Cliff and Phil were best friends, then there was Peanut and Lil Vell on the next street over. All Peanut and Lil Gary would do was steal cars and burn the track up. The police would ride around day and night because they knew someone's car had been stolen. Chris worked at Golden Corral. He would steal raw meat and bring it to Ms. Mabel. Sam would buy some, also. Terrell had just got out of prison. He served four years for robbing a Taco Bell with a knife. Clarence stayed on Dungreen. He had a wife named Me-Me. Clarence was the slickest junkie in the whole hood. He was a professional con-artist. Clarence could cook the shit out of some dope, too.

Then there was Slim. He stayed in a retirement home. It was the same retirement home that Chris stayed in with his mother. Mr. Marshall stayed next door to Lil Gary and Cliff. Mr. Marshall was an old man, he had no family. He retired and bought the duplex across the street. Whoever his tenants were, they never paid. I knew they were mostly women because they gave him sexual favors for their rent. Mr. Marshall was also the candy man. He would sell candy to everyone; the children would usually steal it. He was always pissed off because if someone gave a him $1, they would steal $4 worth.

I would usually sit and talk with him. He always showed me pictures of him on his yacht. He was rich, once upon a time. He kind of reminded me of Mr. Wilson from "Dennis the Menace" except, he was black-Cuban and all the children were his menaces. He was always cussing somebody out and chasing them outside in his underwear for stealing from him. Man, it was a sight. He hardly ever kept candy because he was making no profit. His mind came and went. Sometimes, he talked about his days in the navy, and told me about how he sold tons of kilos. It was impossible to believe, seeing what he had become. But, he did have a lot of pictures to prove it.

Everybody was outside, it was hot as hell, I asked Lil Gary what he had on a sack.

He told me, "10 dollars." I gave him my $10 and he went and found Lil George. Lil George was Los' little brother. Gary made it back with the weed, and we rolled up a blunt and got blowed. Chris was sweating like a slave washing my car. I told Gary it was too hot and I was going inside. As soon as I made it in the house Raegan beeped me, 1,2,3... that was our code. Nothing was going on so I mobbed over to her house. I pulled up, and she was talking about how she wanted some Wendy's. I went and got her some food, came back, grabbed a cigar, and went inside to roll a blunt. I smoked with her momma and brother Cortez. I went into Raegan's room and took a nap.

I woke up around 6 that evening to Raegan's mama's cooking, Damn I was hungry! I couldn't help but feel like I had missed something so I told Raegan to get me a face towel so I could wash my face. I had to go re-up. I jumped in my car and swatted off. I was coming up Chuck and saw

Terrell. I jumped out to rap with him. He was mowing someone's yard, he cut off the lawn mower and walked towards me, I laid back on my car real smooth like the Mac I was, and proceeded to get in his business.

I asked, "What's up Terrell?"
He replied, with his usual stutter, "n, n, no, nothing"
I kept a straight face, all business, then, I asked, "How long have you
been home?"
He said, "Two months."
"Terry told me you were bout it, bout it." Then I

smiled and said, "I know you want some real money."

He said, "I've been h, hi, hitting little li, licks h, here and th, th, there."

I looked at him in disbelief and said, "Yeah right".

I looked up and saw Terry on a Baja. He pulled up on me and Terrell. Terry immediately jumped in Terrell's face like he was mad about something and said, "Give me my money, before I break your jaw, your around here cutting yards and shit!" Terrell never spoked so clear, "M, Mane I'll pay you your money as soon as I get it". Terry was playing with him at first, but then I saw he was getting serious so, I said jokingly, "Terry, Terrell is kind of big now."

Terry said, "I don't care how big this bitch is, I'll break him down."

I laughed and winked at Terry. I said, "Terrell ain't going, he bout it, bout it." Terry smiled, "Goddamn Terrell, you can talk straight when somebody bout to get on your ass huh?" We all laughed.

I got back serious and said, "So, what else you got going on?" Terrell was reluctant to say in front of Terry because he knew he was no joke and everyone must pay sooner or later.

So, all the yards Terrell was cutting, he was actually scoping out his next victim. He went on to tell me about all the shit he could be stealing. I was just the motivation he needed. I explained how the timing was perfect. I told Terrell to come see me later; I had something for him. Plus, we needed to get busy planning everything. I asked Terrell to meet me on Barbwood. Terry pulled up on the bike and jumped in the car with me. I asked him how much money he had. He replied, "About $1500." I said, "Cool." I had about $1800 at the house.

We stopped by the house, then we mobbed to Orange Mound. Ralph was my uncle's son. Ralph smelled just like money all the time. He talked real fast. "What's up lil Cuz?", he asked.

I told him that I needed work ASAP.

Ralph replied "What you trying to do? All I have is already hard, it's good though."

I said, "Give me four Juices, Cuz."

He said, "Damn, lil cuz, you rolling like that out there?" "Y'all buying this shit so fast. I tell you what, everything y'all buy I will front y'all."

I told him I would think about it, and I would get up with him later.

Terry and I jumped in the Cadillac and swatted off. We went back to East Memphis, put the work up, then, drove up to Shoney's. We ordered a T-bone steak and baked potato. While we were sitting down eating, Terry was trying to convince me to take Ralph up on his offer. I told him we already had a good thing going. We didn't owe anyone money and everything we had was ours. Then I said, "It's not like he's gonna give us a whole brick anyways." It seemed like we weren't understanding each other.

After we finished eating we left and went back to the Hood. I was coming up Chuck and saw Bodeen. I asked him where Terrell was. He asked if I needed him to go find Terrell for me. I told him yes and to bring him around to the house. When I pulled up on Barbwood, I was looking for Lil Mark. I wanted to let him know I was straight before he bought a deal from someone else. I went inside the house, grabbed a razor blade and a plate. I was all business.

Lil Mark showed up and made his way into the back room. He said he needed forty rocks. He gave me $400. I really didn't have it like that but, I wanted all money. Plus, I had three more juices so, I was cool. Lil Mark wasn't tripping' anyways. They weren't break downs, they were nice size hoagies. After I got through serving Lil Mark, I stepped outside and saw Bodeen walking up the street; then, a car pulled in the driveway. Terry was moving fast, he beat Lil Mark to the serve. Terry was competitive like that. If someone was trying to quit smoking and get their life together, Terry would give them free Crack, just to keep them on the shit.

When Bodeen came over I asked him where Terrell was. He told me that Terrell was on his way but taking his time. Bodeen just walked off and left him; he was being too slow. Then, Bodeen asked if I needed anything else. He was about to walk to the store for a beer. I told him to bring me a box of cigars. I gave him some money for his beer and the cigars. As soon as I handed Bodeen the money, Chris came shucking and jiving making his way down the street. As soon as he stepped off the curb, Lil Gary turned the corner in a steamer and almost ran Chris's ass over. Chris was so crazy, he fell out and played dead. We all started laughing. Terrell finally made it around the corner. Terrell and I started talking business.

I asked, "When is the best time for him to do these burglaries?" He told me "Sunday, when they go to church."

It was a Friday night and the track was jumping.

I told Terrell, "It's on Sunday, then."

Terrell had $15 on him, and asked if I would serve him. He didn't want me to tell

Terry because he owed him money. So, I hit him like hammer. He seemed surprised by what I gave him and said, "Damn, all that for $15?!" I reassured him that I had him and told him not to nut up on me. He needed to take care of his business. I told him to get whatever was valuable.

Marquette, was Terry's little cousin, she came in the back room and told me Bodeen was outside. I went outside and got my change and cigars from Bodeen.

Bodeen had a Colt 45. Lil Gary and Lil Vell rolled up in this hot ass car. I flagged them down and told them to park the car and come holla at me. I was about to roll a blunt.

Gary said he would be right back he was dropping Vell off. A car pulled up in Sam's driveway. Terry went over there so fast and served Sam's customer before they could even make it up to his door. Then Gary walked up. I motioned him to come over to the car where I was sitting and smoking. Lil Mark was leaving so I asked where he was going. He told me he was going to Clarence's house to serve Me-Me. I knew it was rolling around there because it was Friday, plus, Terry wasn't letting shit get past him. I asked Gary why he was burning the track up with all these hot ass cars. I told him I was trying to make money, and if he kept riding these hot cars through here the police would start coming around. Then, I asked him "Playa, don't you got Nina pregnant?"

He took a toke off the blunt before answering, and said with a breath full of smoke, "Yeah."

I asked him, "Don't you think you need to be trying to get yourself some money?"

He didn't answer.

Money was not his concern, he was too busy fucking these little girls, stealing

cars, and fighting all the time. That was my Lil partner, though. I knew he was solid.

I saw Peanut walking up the driveway. I knew he was with the shit. He was coming to get Lil Gary. He walked up to the car.

I asked him, "What the fuck you want?" I told him the same thing I told Gary, "Stop riding these hot ass cars through here. I'm trying to get some money and don't need the police around"

Peanut just laughed, he wasn't trying to hear shit I had to say.

Then, I purposely tried to get under his skin, and asked him where his fine ass sister was. Gary busted out laughing, Peanut just said "C'mon Gary, let's go". Gary reached for the door handle. I told him before he got out of the car, "Don't let that nut case get you fucked up." He said, " 'aight".

Gary was straight as they come. When our lights were off at the house, he would let me take showers at his house while his parents were at work.

Zo and Lakeisha rode up in his Malibu. He was on

probation. He had two years of paper for the Crack cocaine charge he caught. Zo said, "What's up?" Then him and Lakeisha went in the house. Marie came outside and asked me where Terry was. I told her that I didn't know and asked her "why what's up?" she told me Mack wanted something for the 60 and Honey wanted something for the 20. Of course, she wanted me to give it to her because she was about to do her thing. What I mean by "her thing" is, they would never get exactly what they paid for. She gave them what she wanted them to have. Marie would get them in her room and wouldn't let them leave until they were broke. She was good at making them stay so she could smoke up all their Crack.

Somebody beeped me from Clarence's house, it was Lil Mark, he wanted forty more rocks. I told him to meet me on Barbwood.

He said, "I can't, can you bring it over here?"

I told him, "Okay, but I need a little time because I have to chop 'em down."

He asked, "Can you make them bigger?"

I said, "I'll see what I can do."

I was in the back room chopping down some rocks when Terry walked in. "Have you sold all your dope?", he asked.

"No, but Mark wants forty more rocks."

"Damn where Lil Mark at?" "Over at Clarence' house."

Terry tried again to get me to take Ralph up on his offer. I told Terry I was gonna serve Mark then I was going in the house. I put the rest of the rocks in the bag I had already been serving out of. Terry said he would see me later, and that he was gonna stay down.

I asked Bodeen to ride with me to Clarence's house. I pulled up on Dungreen and pulled in Clarence' driveway. I left the car running and told Bodeen I would be right back. I knocked on the door. Me-Me's fine ass opened the wooden door, then she unlocked the rod iron door. I couldn't help but look at her hips. They were hypnotizing.

Autobiography of Samuel Plain jr.

I asked her where Lil Mark was, she told me he was in the kitchen. Lil Mark had a bankroll. He looked much happier than when he walked off Barbwood. I served like 40 to 50 rocks to Mark. I started to leave and kept staring at Me-Me's gap as she walked in front of me to unlock the door. She was always nice to me, but I never let my guard down, this was Clarence' women. She had game mammy.

Sunday finally rolled around. I was sitting in the house and Marquette ran to me and said, "Somebody named Terrell wants you, Toot". Terrell was in someone's car, he motioned me over to the trunk. He was so excited he couldn't barely get a word out. All I heard was "I'm b, bout it, b, bout it!" He opened the trunk and there was a real bow and arrow set. It had the poisoned arrows and everything! He also had a single shot 12-Gage shotgun made like a pistol, a Tech Nine, and a 22 rifle. He helped me haul all this shit in the back room. I gave him fifteen dime-sized rocks. Terrell was ecstatic! The weeks came and went. It seemed like every Sunday Terrell had ran in somebody's shit and was bringing things through here.

One day, I took my car to Jiffy Lube to get the oil changed. Then I got Raegan; she had a doctor's appointment. On the way back, I noticed my car was running funny. I dropped Raegan off and went back to the house. I was puzzled because my car kept making an unusual tapping sound. It sounded like I threw a rod, but I couldn't have. I thought to myself, "This is the worst motor Cadillac ever made, a 4100, they aren't worth a damn." Turns out I did throw a rod. I called Jiffy Lube to complain, they said they would send a representative out to check it out, I was sick. I told Chris to look

under my car to see if the oil pan bolt was loose. I don't know why I did that. He told me that it was, and this fool tightened the bolt up. Jiffy Lube was at fault for sure, but when their representative came out, Chris had already tightened the oil bolt. It looked as though Jiffy Lube had done everything accordingly, so they didn't take the blame for all my oil leaking out, and causing me to throw a rod. I wanted to kill Chris, I asked him why would he tighten the bolt, I just needed him to see if it was loose! I told him to get the fuck on, before I shot him in his face!

I couldn't help but think later that if I knew that Chris was going to rape a little girl later that summer I would have did something to him. He left bite marks on her butt and vagina. He tricked some little girls to the "Old Folk's Home where him and his mother lived. He told them his mother had some Easter dresses for them. A lot of the girls didn't go. One did, she got raped. The kids in the neighborhood bust out all the windows so his mother had to move for her protection. I never saw Chris again after that.

This shit was so fucked up! No matter how long you know a person, you really never know them. Until they show you who they really are. Now, I needed another car. Which meant, I needed some more money. I needed to re-up. I beeped Ralph, he called me back and told me it would be a few days. So, I called Big E, he told me that he was about to go fuck with his partner and he would come pick me up. I asked him if this dude was straight and he assured me that he was.

I bought six juices and they were already, ready. E. bought three. I had never seen dope this bad in my life! It kept shrinking. No matter what I did. I made what I could from it, but it just kept shrinking. Lil Mark bought some from me, he said the junkies were complaining. Business was super bad. No one was coming through, not to mention, I had no car, and I was stuck with this bullshit! I should have just waited on Ralph.

Bad luck seemed to have no end. Terry did what he could and forced this bad Cocaine on people. It was late at night, Lil Gary told me he had the steamer parked around the corner. I told him to go get it and take me to the house. I was tired, it had been a long day and I did not feel like walking. He got the car and came down the street, but him and Lil Vell rode right past me. At first, I was wondering why he didn't stop. Then, I saw a blue car behind him. It was an undercover police car. Gary rode right through the stop sign, him and Vell jumped out. Their feet had to catch up with the rate the car was going. I saw Gary duck behind a tree, the police jumped out and ran after Vell. Lil Vell ran back toward me on the opposite side of the street. I saw the police catch up with him and put a wrestler clothes line move on him. Terry saw it too. He ducked in the house and grabbed the shotgun. When he came back outside he pointed the gun towards the police officer. That's when I noticed the badge swinging from the officer's neck. I yelled back at Terry "That's the police!". He ducked back in the house and handed the shotgun to Ms. Mabel and grabbed the broom. The other officer immediately drew his weapon and started up the driveway past me. "PUT IT DOWN GODDAMN IT, PUT IT DOWN!" The officer was screaming. Terry went on to explain it was just a broom. The police said, "No I saw it, you had a gun Motherfucker. Where is that gun you had?"

I watched Gary run off into the night. Ms. Mabel came to the door and asked the officer what the problem was, she told the officer all Terry had was the broom, so they let him go. The police asked Vell, "Who is his friend and where does he live?" I heard Vell tell them Gary's name, and pointing he said, "Gary lives right here". I watched the police walk up Gary's driveway and knock on the door. Ms. Clara May answered the door. The police asked if she had a son named Gary and explained that he would have a warrant for his arrest. That's all I heard. The officers told me to go in the house because there was nothing to see.

The next day Terry bought a '76 Coupe Deville Cadillac, it was white with red interior. He bought it from some old white man for $400. Just before Terry bought the white Coupe Deville, he sold the blue '78 Sedan Deville for $1000. The Coupe Deville ran pretty good. It

only needed a radiator. Terry and I were on Barbwood when Terrell walked up. Terrell pulled me off to the side and told me he wanted to show me something. He showed me a
chrome nickel-plated 32 Revolver. I asked him what did he want for it. He said he was gonna keep it, that was going to be his personal gun. He asked if I would hold on to it for him. I said, "Yeah, cool". Terrell told me about his plans to get some money. He was planning on robbing a bank. I told him not to do that because I knew where a real lick was at. He asked with a curious look "Where?"

I told him, "Fast Check".

Then, he said with a stutter, "Y, y, you crazy foo, fool, those A, Arabians will ki, kill me!"

I replied, really quick, "I thought you said you were bout it."

He said "I, I, am, b, but I ain't c, crazy."

I asked him, "How the fuck you plan on robbing a bank?

"Y,y, you'll see", he said, then asked me to front him some Hard.

He promised to pay me back double. I got the pistol from him, put it in my pocket and said "Okay, I got you Terrell." I gave him $40 worth of Crack, he said "Y, you my partner m, main y, you a r, real friend", then he left.

Terry and me jumped in the Coupe Deville and went to get cigars and some Stop Leak for the radiator. When we got to Auto-Zone, we had to sit for a minute because the radiator was steaming hot. We walked in the store and bought the Stop Leak. Stop Leak looks like black pepper. It finds the hole in the radiator and seals it up. This is another lesson I learned from my father. I told Terry "This should work. It shouldn't run hot for a while; until you can get a new radiator." Then I started telling Terry about what Terrell and I had just talked about. Terry said, "Terrell is crazy, he's going to the Penitentiary." I replied, "Yeah, fucking with the Government's money." Then, I said, "There is too much money in the street to be fucking with the Governments money." Terry agreed and said, "Ya dig."

After Auto Zone, we grabbed the cigars and rode back to the hood. It was late at night. I saw Lil Gary. We fired up a blunt and he started explaining to me why he didn't stop last night, and asked if I saw what happened. I told him yeah and

everything that happened after he ran off. I told him Lil Vell's bitch ass told the police everything and they talked to his momma. I also told him about how the officer almost blew Terry's ass off. He passed the blunt back to me in disbelief.

Gary said, pissed off, "I can't believe that soft ass boy told on me."
"The police told your momma they were gonna put a warrant out for your arrest.", I told him.
While I was talking to Gary, Terrell walked up. Terrell gave me $20 and asked for the pistol I was holding onto for him. I went inside, grabbed the gun. I gave him the pistol and asked him what was he about to do. He replied "n, nothing it's on." I went back outside and continued talking to Gary. He told me he was ready to try to get some money. He said he would get a deal from me. He had something he was working on. I told him okay just to holla at me when he got straight.

A few days went by and I hadn't heard back from Terrell. Zo and I were walking in the house, just getting back from the store. I sat down in the living room and started watching T.V. On Channel 5 NEWS, they said, "Up next, a bank robber got away with an undetermined amount of money." As I was paying attention to what they were saying, I saw a video clip of who looked like Terrell wearing a baseball cap, holding a chrome 32 on a bank teller, and demanding money. I called Zo into the living room. The excitement in my voice made Lil Mark come too. I ran outside and told Terry to come in. We were all watching, waiting for the story to come back on. Without a doubt it, was Terrell wearing a baseball cap, robbing a damn bank! Zo immediately started hating

Autobiography of Samuel Plain Jr.

saying, "Ahaa! Y'all thought Terrell was gonna give y'all something. He ain't giving y'all shit!" Lil Mark started laughing and said, "That's most definitely Terrell!" I knew it was him, too. I was sick, I couldn't help but think about how much money he got away with. I told Terry to take me to Raegan's house, I was gonna go take a nap.

On the ride over to Raegan's, Terry and I were talking. I was wondering how much money Terrell had gotten. Terry told me to be patient and that Terrell fucks with me and he's gonna give me something. I told Terry that I hoped he was right. I really needed the money. Even though I tried to talk him out of it, I still hoped Terrell would give me something. I got to Raegan's and laid across her bed. She could tell I had something on my mind, because she asked me what was wrong. I just told her, "Nothing." She asked if I was hungry, I said, "Yeah." Her step dad, Tommy, was barbecuing so she fixed me a plate. I ate, busted a nut, and fell asleep, all in that order.

I was awakened about 11:30 that night to Terry throwing money on me. I asked him, "What's this?"

"Terrell came by.", he said.

I eyeballed the money then I asked, "Where is the rest of it at?" I counted it. It was twenty, twenties. 400 punk ass dollars.
I told Raegan to get me a face towel so I could wash my face. Terry and I
jumped in the Coupe Deville. He burnt rubber all the way up the street. The '76 Coupe Deville came with a 500 engine. That bitch was pulling something serious! I
stayed on Barbwood all night waiting for Terrell to come back. He didn't show up. I continued waiting for him all the next day. It had become nightfall and he finally came. I asked him what kind of bullshit he was on, and where was the rest of the money at. Terrell said, "M, main my f, fat ass b, baby momma!" He told me he hadn't done shit for his two sons in five years and he did the robbery using her car. He told me he was gonna rob

Autobiography of Samuel Plain jr.

another bank early in the morning and that he needed a ride to his baby momma's house. I asked him what time and he told me to be up about 7 in the morning. I agreed.

Terry dropped me off at Raegan's house about 11:30 that night. I fell asleep, then woke up about 6 o'clock the next morning. I beeped Terry. He hadn't been to sleep that night. He was still up, and came to pick me up. We got on Barbwood. Terry already had a blunt rolled up. It was getting close to 7:00. I couldn't believe it. I saw Terrell coming up the street. He was actually on time! We all jumped in the Coupe Deville and went to Terrell's baby's momma's house. We dropped him off, then me and Terry went to Waffle House for breakfast.

We had T-bone's and eggs, of course. I was tired as hell. I told Terry to drop me off at Raegan's and I would catch up with him later. I fell asleep. Terry beeped me, it was about 4 that afternoon. I called Terry back, and he told me Terrell was at the house waiting on me. He asked if I wanted him to come pick me up. I told him, "No, I will be there in 10 minutes." I jumped up, brushed my teeth, and washed my face. Of course, Raegan came up to me and was trying to hold me up. I told her I was in a hurry. I ran across Goodlett to Sheffield High School. I jogged all the way across the field. I came up on a car in the Vocational School parking lot. A guy and girl were in the car making out. I told the guy I would give him $5 to take me to Barbwood. This guy was too busy trying to get some pussy. He told me "No." But his girlfriend told him that Barbwood was only right up the street and it was worth $5. He said "I ain't taking him!" His girl snapped, "Boy I'm hungry, you better take him!" So, dude reluctantly said "Ok", and gave me a ride. When we pulled up on Barbwood I told dude, "Right here; I'm cool" and gave him the 5 bucks. I hopped out the car and saw Terry and Terrell standing under Ms. Mabel's carport.

We all went in the back room. Terrell seemed nervous; I think it was Terry that was making him nervous. Terrell

Autobiography of Samuel Plain Jr.

handed me a bankroll. It was $5000. I counted the money, and asked him where the rest was at. He said that was all he had got, I knew he was lying. He said that he wanted to party, and asked if I would give him something. He was nervous. I gave him a quarter ounce of crack. I wanted to keep him close because I wanted to find out where the rest of his money was at. I asked Honey if she wanted some beer, she said "Sure!" So, she and Marie hopped in the car with Terry, Terrell, and me.

Terrell bought beer, cigarettes, and two bags of ice. He also got a hotel room on Lamar. Once they got settled in the room, Terry and I left. When Terry and I got back to the hotel, Honey and Marie were knocked the fucked out! They must have partied hard, they smoked themselves to sleep! I thought Terrell had murdered them and left. Terry and I woke them up. There was a little beer left, not much. We were all on the way out of the room when Terrell pulled back up in a red Nissan Sentra, he was playing Master P's song I'm Bout It, Bout It real loud. He had two guys with him I had never seen before. They were from Chicago. And that's how Terrell introduced them. I was reluctant to meet anybody. Terrell had some more money, because he bought a car, and he told these guys about my lick. I told Terrell he was going to jail in that red ass car, with the Temporary Tag in the back window. Plus, his face was all over the NEWS. He should have done the right thing with the money and gave it all to me. I told him I didn't want any part of what he was talking about doing, and I sure didn't want any part of the two clowns, he had with him. I told Terry, "Let's roll." I was so pissed off, but I couldn't talk in front of Marie and Honey. We rode back to the hood. I told Terry to take me by my house. I told Melody that I had $2,700 =for the light bill. She smiled. How I loved to see her smile. The light bill was super high. Because we had been stealing lights before Memphis LGW, cut the line from the pole to the house.

I got 3 1/2 juices with the rest of the money. Everyday

Autobiography of Samuel Plain jr.

Terrell would come and beg me for Hard in that stupid red ass car, bumping Bout It, Bout It. Now that the lights were back on in the house, I was watching TV, when someone knocked on the door, it was Terrell. He started telling me, "Ma, main I Fu, fucked up, I, I should have lis, listened to y, you!"

I asked him, "How much money did you really get?" He replied, "It's n, not imp, p, portant."
I said, "I told you not to rob no bank Mane. Now that your ass ran out of

money, you came back to Earth, huh?" He just looked at the ground.

I told him that I heard he has been buying dope from everybody in the hood, and that everybody knows he bought that dumb ass car with the bank money. He asked again if I would give him some Hard. I told him to hold on, I gave him a $20 rock. He said "Wh, wh, what's this!" I told him I was fucked up, and he was fucked up worse than me because he was going to jail. I said to him now neither one of us had any money.

I felt so bad watching him leave. All those weak ass dudes he was buying dope from didn't care what happened to him. All the junkies he was getting high with only cared about getting high. He just wouldn't listen. That was the last time I saw him free.

Zo and Lil Mark were laughing at first, then they found out Terrell had given me some money. Of course, they stuck their hands out. Zo came and picked me up in his Malibu. The whole hood was blocked off. We couldn't turn down Chuck Street, so, we rode down a little further, and we were able to turn down Wooddale. It was so ironic, as soon as I got to Wooddale and Austin Wood, I saw FBI Agents in Terrell's mother's yard. I watched his momma walk up to the FBI Agents. It's one of those moments that are still frozen in my mind. The Agent was showing her a picture. I guess he was asking her if it was her son. I saw her nod her head as we drove by. It was unbelievable. I remember feeling bad for her.

Of course, Zo started talking about "I'm glad you didn't give me any of that money!" I told him, I really wasn't trying to hear that shit and said, "At first, you were hating and wanting some money. Now, you supposedly glad you didn't get any." He couldn't say shit because he knew I was telling the truth. He said he was going to Durby Circle because the 'Hood was too hot. We rode over to Durby Circle. I stayed over there for a while but I had Crack to sell, I said to myself, Fuck it, I didn't go in the bank and get any money. So, I wasn't worried about the shit. I called Terry to come pick me up and take me back to the hood. The whole hood was talking about the FBI being at Terrell's mommas house. And the police were looking for him high and low. I stayed on the track all that night. Early that morning about 6 am an unmarked police car pulled up. They pulled in Lil Gary's driveway, got out, and knocked on the door. They went inside and got Gary. He was sleeping. It was the same officers he ran from a weeks ago. They put him in the back of their car a rode off.

    I felt sorry for Gary and Terrell, but I had my own issues to focus on. I needed a car, I got sick of hopping rides. I had seen a mint green '77 Sedan Deville for sale down the street from my Auntie Ellen's house. I really didn't want it, but, like I said, I needed a car. I went and talked to the White couple who owned it. I offered them $500 for it. The guy seemed excited and said he took it. The car apparently had been sitting there and no one was interested in it. It ran pretty good. It needed a fuel pump, though. I took it to Steve, and let him put a fuel pump on it for me. Steve could build a car from stretch. The car ran perfect! I think the White guy thought it needed a carburetor, but it only needed the fuel pump. Things had started looking up for me. Lil Gary got out the next day. He told me that the police kept asking him how did he get away and where did he run to when he got out of the car. Gary said he just laughed at them. Then he asked me if I heard about Los getting out.

I told him "No. When did he get out?"

He told me "About a week ago."

Zo came outside and asked Terry to use his car. Terry was reluctant to

give him his keys, but he gave them to him anyway. Zo left. We were all in the house when Zo started knocking on the window.

He said, "Toot you have a Driver's License, come get the car for me. I was in an accident, I've been drinking and I'm on probation."

I told him "I'm not going anywhere. "You're not gonna to get me fucked up this

time.

Zo was so drunk he had torn up everyone's car on the street! He hit eight parked cars going down the street. By the time him and Terry made it back to the car, the police rode up on them. They were pushing the car back. Terry told them that he was driving. They didn't arrest him; they just gave him a ticket. Terry told them he had fallen asleep at the wheel. The Cadillac was frowned up, but still had a good motor and transmission. When they made it back, they told me everything that had happened. I was glad I didn't go with them.

The next day, I saw Los. He saw the car and said "Damn, what happened to this Motherfucker?" I told him what happened. He said he needed a car, and I told him the green car was for sale. I said I wanted $700 for it. He said he wanted it and to let him test drive it. He test-drove it and came back. He told me to give him two weeks because he wanted it. I told him that was cool. This gave me time to find something else to ride in.

Terry was so mad at Zo for wrecking his car. Plus, Terry had to pay for the people's cars that had been hit. Whatever chance of getting a Driver's License was lost for real. A Officer was rolling down Barbwood when Peanut decide to start shooting at his Police car. He called for back-up, immediately. They hit the cut and ran on Brentwood. In no time, police were everywhere. Two days later Peanut was in a Steamer when Officer Rick spotted him. Peanut tried to out run the police, they made Peanut flip the car. He was lucky because Officer Rick was trying to kill him. Officer Rick was known not only in Memphis, but throughout the nation. Mainly because he was on HBO. The show was about police that had killed in the line of duty. He was the same police that had told us that if we get hit by one of those 45 shells it was over. Clem owed me $1200 on the 1st of the month. He was so good you could give him one rock and charge him $300 for it. He would run up a $1500 tab with you, but he always paid. Los had $400. I told him I would keep the Title till he paid me the rest of my money. I let him have the car and explained I may need him to take me somewhere every now and then. He said, "Cool, I fuck with you." It seemed odd that the car that I needed so bad, wasn't mine anymore. I kind of regretted it, though. As soon as that Los got rolling good all he did was roll past me. It was cool all I wanted was my money. Plus, I was on my grind something serious.

August 16, 1997. I never will forget this day because I got into two different car accidents. Los came through, so, Zo, Terry, and I jumped in the car. Los told me to drive because I had a license. I asked him about my money he told me he's going to pay me next week. We were on our way back to the hood when this car pulled out in front of me. I had to think fast. I had two choices: hit the breaks or hit the gas. I chose to hit the gas. At that very moment, I was passing Los the blunt. I looked up and it was too late to stop! I hit this car so hard it wrapped itself around a pole and span up it, then came down. Cars started to pull over. The Cadillac was still running. I got out. I was so scared I thought I had killed someone, plus, the car smelled just like weed. All the witnesses said they barely missed the car. Everyone was ok, thank goodness.

Then, all of a sudden, I heard glass breaking out of the car I hit. Then this stupid man that had pulled out in front of me comes out saying "Where did she go?" Terry clicked screaming, "I'll kill you bitch ass." Los and I grabbed Terry. I was so happy he was alive. Damn, I thought whoever was in that car was dead. The police got our information and we left.

I got a ride to Raegan's house and had told her what happened. As usual, she was hungry. So, one of Cortez friends took me to Wendy's. Now, here is why I

remember this day so well. I got Raegan's food and we on our way back when this fool gets the bright idea to go around a car on the left-hand side. I saw it happen in slow motion. The car turned left and hit us as we were passing it. This sent us spinning up into on-going traffic; good thing there were no cars coming. Now, him and his girlfriend were scared and screaming, but he was showing out just a minute ago driving fast. I had just been through this so I was very calm. I could have killed this Asshole. The car finally stopped spinning and hit the curb then he tried to drive away. I said, "If your hoe ass moves this car with me in it again. I'm going to fuck you up!" I got out the car and started to walk back when I noticed that this little kid that hit us, had just started driving. Cortez's friend bitch ass hopped out the car like it was lil dude's fault. By this time, I didn't care. I kept mobbing. When I made it to Raegan's house I told her what had happened. Then, she had the nerve to say I was over exaggerating! I cursed her ass out and left. I didn't know what God was trying to tell me, but I was shook.

I walked back on Barbwood where someone could relate. I told Terry what had happened, Zo said, "We need to go to the hospital." I asked were Los was because since he thought we all needed to go, then we ALL needed to go. We all went to the hospital and Los met us up there. The guy I hit had insurance. They paid me for my car and gave me a rental car. They gave me $1500 for the Cadillac. Los was mad but its his own fault he should've paid me for my car, and got his Title. The rental car was a Neon coupe. The first day I got the rental car, I went to Cory B. Trott's office to sit and talk with him about my case. He asked me who all was in the car when I got into the wreck. I told him, and he gave all of us a doctor to see. I asked him about my vehicle and he told me that he would give me a call back. I told him that the man I hit had insurance with All-State and they're paying for my rental car. How about Terry, Lil Gary and I were on our way to go get some work in the Neon when we got into another accident. A head on collision. It seemed as though I was accident prone. Bert saw the wreck happen. He ran out into the street to see if we were ok. He called Ralph and told him I was in an accident. Ralph pulled up talking fast, as usual, "Lil cuz, you aight?" I had hit an old lady and her son. They were ok, though, but the police gave me a ticket. As soon as we hit that car I saw Terry's head about to hit the dash board when all of a sudden, the air-bag came out. I put my arm up to cover my face before the air-bag jumped out. It cut my arm up pretty bad and it was swollen. This powder stuff came out and it woke me up. I asked if everyone was ok. Gary said, "I'm straight." Then, Terry finally came to after I called his name a few times.

They towed the Neon. I didn't give a fuck I had quarter key fair. Ralph served me nine ounces and gave us a ride back to the 'hood. We talked about him fronting me some work. That's when he told me I didn't have to buy it anymore, he had me.

I said "Cuz, I'm straight I'll let you know." I could tell he was checking out the real-estate.

Terry said, "Why u didn't tell him yes?"

I said, "Be cool. His price isn't right. If he starts to give us work every time he gets it then we would depend on him."

Terry replied, "But if we got work all the time we would sew up the whole hood." I said, "True, but what he's trying to do is get us to push his pack for him."
Terry still tried to convince me to take the deal. I pointed out to him "You see
    he didn't match the nine we just bought."

Autobiography of Samuel Plain jr.

I headed in the house to chop down two ounces. I served deals and one for-
ones all day. By this time, it was 4am, time to shut down shop. I headed to Waffle House on American Way and got me a T. Bone steak. After I had downed my whole pack, Terry and I talked some more about Ralph's offer. Terry won me over on the idea. He said all we had to do was use their money to buy more work on the side. Only thing was, I had inherited a bad genes. The honest Abe gene. It's almost always impossible for me to lie about anything. On the other hand, this shit was a gift for Terry. He would lie about everything with a straight face.

I pulled up on Bey Street in The Mound. I saw Tim and Ralph on the porch talking when I pulled up. Ralph said "Wassup, little Cuz I been waiting on you." I gave Tim some dap and headed inside. Bert had two bricks already ready. There were four keys of soft on the table. In total six bricks. I never had saw this much work in my life. Of course, he gave me the work that had already been cooked. 9 juices ready. His whip game was crazy.

Bert was a cooking motherfucker. He would take return and a cloths hanger and make two ounces four and half like it wasn't shit. He gave Tim nine onions, too. All this was extra work he had whipped up. Of course, I asked for some powder. He wasn't going for that, though. He gave me a look like, don't push it, and I didn't. Bert had two bodies at the time. Let's just say I knew of two bodies. This guy was no joke. I mobbed back to East Memphis real smooth, beeped Terry and told him the Eagle had landed. He knew that meant I was at the house.

I heard his bike hit the ground. Terry, never used the kick stand on his bike for shit. I unlocked the door and showed him the work. He was ecstatic. We downed nine ounces so fast and was asking for more. The first pack was gone in two days. All I sold was deals and one for one. Barbwood was a rolling track that Terry and I had crunk up years ago. It was easy. All you needed was some work to sale and you could actually get rich. Lil George had this motherfucker rolling too with the weed. George was getting like ten pounds when he was 14 years old. I was back on now.

My birthday was coming up. Master P dropped Ghetto Dope. I had a White on White '91 Sedan Deville. Ralph was having a birthday party in The Mound. His birthday was two days before mine. I was turning 19yrs old and had a baby girl on the way. Ralph party was off the chain. Everybody in The Mound was there. Ralph and Bert was so happy to see me. They couldn't give me enough work. Terry was a hustling motherfucker. Terry loved selling crack. I hated it. It wasn't for me. It was just was a means to an end.

The party was everything I needed. Champagne all night long. I had so much fun. All the Cougars there where all over me. They knew who was getting money and who

wasn't. There was so much champagne everyone had a glass. It's was a real celebration. I had a lot to be thankful for. We balled hard that Winter like the money was never going to stop.

After my birthday, it started to get cold. It would be Winter soon, but at least Barbwood was rolling. I was running through packs like a motherfucker. When I first started to move work, I got the understanding that if you sell fast, it didn't matter what you sold it for, as long as you could keep getting it. And, of course, you had to have someone that wanted to buy it. Now this was my dilemma. Ralph wanted an arm and a leg for his work because he was fronting it to me. I could either purchase it from someone else at a cheaper price, or continue to get it from him because he was fronting it to me.

But I was business minded. So, we would buy work with the money we made off Ralph money. I was doing a little bit more than just maintaining. I was getting over like a fat ass cat. I gave Terry my white on white '91 Sedan Deville. I had a '91 Cadillac Seville. It was the color of Champagne with plum red seats. I loved this car. When you started it the would say, "Good Morning, Monitoring Systems are OK." I had to personalize it. You know, make it mine. That means I had to put rims on it. Bodeen brought this guy to me. That had some rims for sale. I could tell this dude was desperate. Now, the first thing I had to do was separate him and Bodeen. Bodeen was with the shit. He was scheming from a crackhead perspective. When I asked how much this guy wanted, Bodeen beat the guy saying a $1,000. I said real smooth, "Stay out my business Bodeen." He continued with his rhetoric. That's when I looked at the guy and said "I guess he's going to buy them then." I thought this man was going to shit his pants when I walked off. I winked at Bodeen and said gone and grab those joints dog.

Dude said "Man, how much you'll give me for them. That's when I asked, "Where you get them from?"
He looked reluctant, but said, "Man I was trying to get $600."

I said "Yeah, right. I'll give $400 for them. Take it or get that hot ass shit away from here."
Bodeen was hot. I didn't give a fuck. Dude took the $400. I told Bodeen I take care of him when he was done putting them on. The rims where made like the Sun was shining with Gold Cadillac amulets on brand new 16-inch Vogue tires. Once Bodeen had the tires on, I got him to wash my car for me. This was a beautiful automobile. I gave him a hoagie. The biggest rock I could find in my sack. He wasn't pleased with what I had given him. So, I reassured him that Terry would take care of him later.

Honey saw me give Bodeen that rock. She also saw the size of it. She made sure Bodeen wasn't going anywhere. This became a problem as the day went on. Bodeen kept asking me, "Give me something Mane?" I told him that was all I had and that Terry had something. He was reluctant to ask Terry anything and he had a good reason. He knew Terry wasn't going to give him shit. I did, too, that's why I told him to ask Terry. By this time, he was sprung out with no money. I told him, "I gave you that to

Autobiography of Samuel Plain Jr.

sell not smoke,

fool. My game was the best. See I don't lie. I just give the option that you never thought of.

With the traffic plus Terry car and my car, the police started to watch us. It was almost impossible for me to drive anywhere in East Memphis without the police following me. Once I left the hood they would back off. They would follow me in Undercover cars then turn off down another street. Out of nowhere, a Blue and White police car would appear and pull me over and put me in the back of the car. The same Undercover officers would pull up and search my Cadillac. I never got use to this. How could you ever get used to being violated?

The police would sit outside on Barbwood and watch the house. People that did come by didn't get anything from us because we wouldn't sell them shit. If we did, they had to smoke it in the house. They watched Sam's house, too. The Memphis Police had this operation called "Zero Tolerance." I survived this shit without a case. They could not harass us forever.

Bowlegged Luke, told Terry he knew an old White lady in Mississippi that had some rims on her car. Terry told him he would give him $1500 for them. Luke agreed and left. We saw Luke on the NEWS. He had put the police on a high-speed chase in Mississippi. The police shot up the woman's car. Luke got shot, but he was still living. The State Troopers put spikes in the road. This made the car flip multiple times. Once the car landed in the woods they shot it up hitting Luke in the back. Luke got 15yrs for this carjacking charge.

November was here and Raegan was over-due by a week. I was thinking she was never going to come out. I got the call I had been waiting on my whole life. Raegan's mama was on the other end saying, "Toot, get up we on our way to the hospital. Raegan's having the baby." I jumped up. It was about 5:30 in the morning, November 19,1997. I turned the shower on as I was brushing my teeth. I just needed a hot shower to wake me all the way up. I got dressed and walked out the door. The hawk that was outside made me rethink about what I had on. I started my car and ran back in the house. I grabbed my coat and told Melody that Raegan was in Labor. She was getting ready for work. It was extremely cold outside. Raegan stayed in labor all day long. For most of the day it was just Raegan, her mother and me at the hospital. By the time she was ready to give birth, everyone was at the hospital. All of her family was there.

Terry and Anthony came to the hospital after Poo was born. They put everyone out except me and Raegan's mother. I watched the doctor cut her with a scalpel from her vagina to her butt. At this point I had to go out the room. I came back in though. The doctor put a suction cup on top of my baby's head and pulled. I thought to myself, "What the fuck are they doing to her head?" And then she started to slide out. I saw her shoulders. Then it was like she just slid right out. She was so long. I was in shock for sure. I thought they would never stop pulling her out. She didn't cry. The sound she made was as if she was talking. That's when the doctor said, "We have a talker." I remember looking at her like how could I be a part of making something so perfect. 7 pounds, 6 ounces, and 21 1/2 inches long. There are no words to explain how I felt in

that moment. Here I was, only 19 years old and the father of an amazing little girl. She was absolutely, perfect! All the food runs to Wendy's, stomach rubs, and even the arguments me and Raegan had was all worth it. I couldn't be prouder of Raegan for giving me something so special. Raegan and I had stopped arguing so much. This was short-lived, though.

It wasn't even Christmas yet and me and Raegan where fighting, again. Destiny was so small, like a month old. I was trying to sleep and Raegan wouldn't let me. At this point in our relationship, she had a problem with everything I did. Hell, she already had the best part of me let her tell it. So, I guess there was nothing else I could give her. We loved each other very much. Our relationship gave us a beautiful daughter. Then came to a end. Which made us have a better friendship so that we could be able to co parent.

Winter of '98

It was so cold, but having a family that was growing made me feel warm. Destiny was two and half months when my sister gave birth to a baby boy. January 31, 1998. I couldn't believe it. Our family was growing. When we were kids, I never thought those days would bring these days. I was a father, and my sister was a mother. I showed Destiny her cousin. I didn't stay at the hospital long. I dropped her off with Raegan.

Earlier that day, before my sister called, I got Vince to take me to The Mound to get straight. Vince had a truck with handyman equipment in the bed of it. He would lay the letter on a couple of buckets. That way it could be seen without it being a traffic violation. This dude had hats and some more shit. He was a high bituminous driver. So, he kept this type of shit going on. Orange Mound was hot as a motherfucker. Police were everywhere. We pulled up on Bey Street. As I got out the car, Bert was coming down the steps. He dapped me up. Then he jumped in his green Lexus on gold rims. Damn he was hurting. I watched him spank off like a jet. Vince was starting the process of getting his truck to looking like a working man's truck. I walked in the house to see Ralph doing business. He looked up and said, "Wassup Lil cuz?" He was smelling like money as usual.

Ralph was busy as hell. The pack had just touched down. I was hopeful that he had put mine to the side. He did. Ralph always looked out for me. I grabbed it and was on my way out the door when Ralph called me back and told me it's going to go fast. Just waiting on me. He was going to blessed me with more next time. Vince was looking nervous as usual. Main why your weak ass always looking so scary. I laughed he was all business. Put your seatbelt on. That's what made me laugh even harder. He

was a funny motherfucker. He handed me a painting hat with paint all over it. We look just like working man.
Vince smoked primos. I never actually saw him hit a pipe. We pulled up at the house. Terry was watching TV waiting on us. I told him to give Vince something for taking me. That's when my sister called. I had no idea what was going on in the 'hood. Barbwood

was jumping. Cars were everywhere like it was the 1st of the month. The track be funny like that. Sometimes it's slow then sometimes it's super-fast. When the track is fast there's a lot of shit going on.

Everyone had been waiting on this work to hit. I couldn't get word in with Terry to see what was happening. When he got time, he told me that this was not going to last and that we need more. "I'll call Ralph", Terry said. "Toot, I got somebody that's straight. Let's grab something", he continued. That's when I told him what Ralph said. We didn't have time to flip the money. It seemed like forever. I had been spending money like there was no tomorrow. I had got so use to having it and not having to look for it.

Two weeks went by, still nothing. Then the most fucked up shit happened. Bert got caught at the greyhound bus station with 6 kilos of cocaine. They said he had got away but tried to get the bag off the bus anyway. I should have listened to Terry. I hated selling rocks. I had no choice. "Fuck this shit", I thought. "I got to hit me a lick."

I knew just who to call. I hadn't told anyone about this lick. Only Terry. I told someone I trusted to do the job. Andrew was a robber. All he did was rob. He didn't sell drugs. He was an aggravating robbery type of guy. Dangerous as hell. I decided to tell him everything about the lick because it was happening. Fuck this being broke shit.

It became a job. Every day I would watch as they opened and carried a bag of money in. See, if you do your homework it will pay off. At 6:50 every morning they would pull up and open the store. Sometimes people would be waiting in cars for the store to open. Especially in the Winter time. It was cold so, you couldn't see in the cars because ice would be all over the windows. No one could see you sitting there with a mask on. There was no armored car picking up the money. So, this only meant one thing, they were handling the cash themselves.

The store owner always kept a gun on his side. Andrew was glad he had a gun. That made it interesting. Andrew told me he had a man that he would use for the job. I was cool with that. I had a new perspective on robbing. I watched the whole thing take place. We were there before the store opened, 5 minutes before they arrived. See, homework pays off. If we were there any longer, the car's windows would have unthawed and you would have been able to see inside. Plus, their car wasn't the only car waiting for the store to open.

The store owner got out his truck with his gun in one hand and his bag in the other. His cousin that worked at the store was unlocking the door. Andrew walked up behind him and grabbed the man hand and pointed his gun at the store owner opening the door. His partner pointed his gun at the store owner holding the gun. It was the perfect ambush. The store owner dropped the bag and his gun.

As they pulled off the store owner picked his gun up and started to fire off rounds at the car as it sped off. I watched the action from across the street. The lick was for $50,000! This was where everyone in the 'hood went cash their checks. The store owner didn't believe in American banks. He carried a bag of money in that store every day. No one had never tried him. Terrell kept saying he a killer. We Knocked his

ass off for 50,000. I met up with Andrew later that day. He gave me $2,000. Him and his friend gave me a thousand dollars apiece. I learned fast if you wanted the big money, you have to take the same risk.

Atlanta Freak Nik was in two weeks. All the heavy dope boys in the town that really was having work was going to Atlanta. That made dope prices go up. I took those $2,000 and got busy. Terry was selling his own work. I had to get to hustling. My Seville needed a transmission. I wasn't about to get it fixed. On to the next one. Andrew picked me up in a White on White El Dorado. I had been swinging like Tarzan. I had a bankroll to go to the Freak Nik.

We stayed in Atlanta three days. I don't think we slept one. It was so much traffic that we didn't leave anything in the hotel room. Because it was impossible to get back to it. What I remember most is all the girls from different States and how they would say, "You are country, but sexy." It seemed like every female I talked to said the exact same thing. There were people from Virginia, South Carolina, North Carolina, Alabama, Texas, Arkansas, Illinois, Kansas, Oklahoma, Indiana, Kentucky, Louisiana, Mississippi, Tennessee...

It was a big party in the streets of Atlanta. All day, every day. Everywhere was crunk. This was the last one, as a matter of fact. I thought about Bert getting fucked up at the bus station because if Bert was out, I know we would have been doing some big boy ass shit.

We were cleaned as fuck in the EL Dog, representing this Memphis shit. But those Atlanta guys was getting real money. Those young guys were riding Benz's and BMW's and looking like they could stand one. A robbery that is. It was so much traffic that helicopters kept filming it. At night, the helicopters would shine there lights on the traffic. I guess for the nightly Newscast. It was a Waffle House on every corner in Atlanta. They were all Crunk as fuck.

When I got back to Memphis, I had a different mindset. I wanted it all. I wasn't going to leave nothing to chance. I missed my baby girl. This was the first time I had been away from her this long. We were each other's universe. She jumped out of her mother's arms with excitement when she saw me. Her little feet kicking up a storm. "Who did it?", I asked. She put her mean mug on to let me know she was still down. I burst out laughing. Every time I asked her this, she would make the same face. It had become our 'little thing.'

I stayed in traffic all over Memphis. Our weekends were very busy. On Sundays, we would ride through Riverside Park and hit Crystal Palace later that day, Beale Street on Fridays and Saturdays, and the Mirage on Fridays, Saturdays, and Sundays, and then D&D Sundays again. Just flexing in traffic fucking with females. I had no time to sell work nor was I interested in it.

That lawsuit finally hit. I went Corey B. Trotz Law Firm. He had a check for $2000. I put a Grand with it. Sam had A-1 credit, so, I got him to sign for me a car. We went to Cadillac of Memphis. I saw a gorgeous Seville. White Diamond. This was a beautiful car. They wanted close to 30,000 for it. The car note was $550, not including

insurance. He put the car on his insurance so I could drive it off the lot. Mane you couldn't tell me shit. See things are easy to get but sometimes hard to maintain. Everyone was hating on me. Sam stayed on my ass about the insurance. Shit, I had to sell some work to get some money. I gave my pack to Lil Yo and told him when he run out, to down my pack. He was taking turns serving out his sack and mine. I wasn't re-ing up at all. I was just spending money. Balling like a motherfucker.

Sam was worrying the shit out of me about this insurance. One day I was on Beale Street and my car wouldn't start. The battery was corroded. I called Sam and told him what the car was doing. This was as good as he wanted it.

He said, "That motherfucker going back tomorrow. It won't start. I dare them sale me a piece of shit like that."

"It's running fine now.", I said.

"No, it quit in less than a month. That motherfucker going back. Yeah, meet me at 9:00am in the morning.", he argued.

Cadillac of Memphis didn't cut checks so we had to go to Bud Davis Cadillac. I was sick as fuck. I was back where I started. No car and back on Barbwood every day, trying to make a dollar out of 50 cents.

Sam was so fucking happy I was out that car. I was too. He was worrying the shit out of me about some damn insurance. He could have put me on his insurance. But it's cool just some more motivation. I had to get back focus on some money.

I mobbed on Brentwood. Lil George and Cedric was shooting dice so I jumped in the cramp game. I won like $200. I quit with my winnings and mobbed back on Barbwood. When I got back, I saw Andrew. I told him they were gambling. He said "What they shooting." I told him $20. He was going to gamble. I said, "Cool", and walked in the house.

About an hour later Andrew called on the house phone. He told me he started to lose his money and he called Big Key to get his money back. But Big Key didn't shake nothing. So, he had upped the pistol on lil George and Cedric. He robbed them for their jewelry and money. Now Cedric GD so he got his money back. George was neutral. George brother was GD which was Los. Andrew was GD too, so, this cause all kinds of shit. They didn't want no problems. They started to politic. I got so tired of hearing "Folks, Folks, Folks." GD's came by the bus load, trying to get George stuff back. It was all GD business until they pulled a gun on Terry and tried to rob him. Terry wouldn't give Bart shit.

I called Andrew and told him what had happened. He said he was on the way to East Memphis. Once he made it, we all mobbed to Danville Square. I knocked on the door. Tanya said, "Who is it?" I said, "Toot." All the lights in the house went off.

She opened the door and said, "Don't start nothing Toot, my kids are inside."

I said, "You know I'm not trying to bring no problems to your house Tanya, where Bart at?"

Now Bart has always been my friend. He was George

cousin though. He was upset about what happened. It's funny how all that cool shit went out the window so fast. As so as they came outside everybody started upping their guns. This was GD land. It was so many GD's over here. It's was a stand-off.

I said, "Damn, when we start robbing each other. We been getting money without all this shit going on."

Bart said, "We going to keep robbing until my kin folks get his jewelry
back."

I said, "You see how this shit going. Somebody going to get killed.
That's when I notice this dude with him was anxious. I couldn't see us making it out this situation alive. The GD's was coming from everywhere. They were on the roof
with guns. We were surrounded.
The dude with Bart said, "Who going to get killed?" I was calm because
I knew who I was about to kill.
I repeated, "Like I said, we been getting money without all this. I know
y'all will shake something. Like y'all know we'll shake something. So, keep someone from getting killed let's just stay getting money."
We all backed up. Zo kept his gun on the man on the roof as we made our
next move. Zo walked beside the car until we were in the clear. That never happened. It was so many men with guns. They were just waiting on 'the word.'
We finally made it out of the apartments. We went to the house. Andrew said he felt bad about what he had gotten me involved in. He decided to go back. Like I said it was GD business. He came back just in time to tell us that there was a blackout swat headed our way. He gave them the pawn shop ticket. Their beef was no more after that.

I later learned the blackout swatted was GD's. This was the people they used to do their murders. I was glad this bullshit was over with. It had been a long week full of bullshit. Plus, my reputation was being ruined. It was getting harder for me to buy work. Because people knew I was hanging out with the robbers.

I went downtown to 201 popular to see Bryan. He was in jail so you could only see him through the glass. You had to talk to him on a phone. We were having a good conversation when someone come and told me that someone wanted me. I got up to see who it was and to my surprise it was Terrell. Damn, Bryan was hot because me and Terrell had a lot to talk about.

I asked him had he been getting the money I gave his mama. He said, "Yeah." I went on to tell him that his mama told me to keep my money. God has him now. Terrell said, "Yeah he he he does." I said, "Mane you getting soft. That's when the Officer said visiting time was up. I gave Terrell the house number to call me.

I ran back to tell Bryan to call me, but he was already going through the door to Hell. Damn I was glad to get the fuck out of there. It was good to see Bryan and Terrell though.

It was time for me to get a car and I knew just the one I wanted. I had my eye on a green, '95 Z2-8. Now this was a fun car. The police in the hood called it a Hotrod. I hoped the deal go through on it. Hopefully, my man would find a bank that will approve it. Edward was the man, when it came to getting a bank loan. He had everyone in town riding slick in some up to date type shit, so, of course I got it.

I kept the Z-28 about 50 days. My man on inside told me I was putting too many miles on it and that he was going to put me in something else. This cocksucker gave me a '95 Hyundai Sonata. White with tinted windows. He told me it was temporary and not to worry because they would be getting some more cars next week.

He called me two days later to tell me the deal was done. He had gotten me approved. When I got there, I could tell he was with the shit saying things like, "Look, you're a first-time buyer, plus, you're only 19yrs old Keep the car six months. Build you some credit. Then I can put you in anything you want."

Before I could say anything, he handed me a check for $1,500. I had put $2,500 down on the Z-28. He had gotten me approved for a $1,000. I still didn't want this girl car. The note was $225. One good thing had come of all this, the bank had given me a try.

I thought at this point nothing could make my day go any worse. I had to give back my car and get a girl's car in return. But, things turned from bad to worse. That buying a car I didn't like was the least of my worries because the news I got next was devastating.

Terry beeped me and said that Peanut had gotten killed at Sheffield School. I told Edward I had to go and I would sign the papers tomorrow. I raced back to the 'hood. I parked at Raegan's house. There was a crowd of people outside and high school kids and parents were everywhere. I moved through the crowd to see Peanut's cap laying under the tree. His body, nearby, lie lifeless. Someone grabbed Peanut and put him in the headlock only to release a lifeless body. They had shot him in the head five or six times. At his Wake, I could see where the bullets entered the top of his head and exited out of the back of his head by his neck. It's strange because he had just gotten out of jail and was trying to change. Just because he changed doesn't mean his enemies changed, though. His poor mother showed us what he had highlighted in his Bible before he was murdered. It's almost like he knew he was going to die that afternoon. Things tried to get back normal. Edward had given me the paper work to the deal. I signed it. I didn't care about having a girl car, at the moment. I would ride this wherever I wanted.

That $1500 went pretty fast with me not trying to flip it. So, it was time to get more money. Andrew and I got together at his apartment we were talking about our next move. I had the Tag numbers we needed to get the address where the money was coming from. I made sure to get his wife's tag numbers, too. It would be a week or so before we heard anything.

I was in the Barbershop. When I saw two Arabian kids come in to get a haircut. The Arabian guy had a gun on his side. He sat down with the boys as they got their

haircut. The barbershop was crowded. I usually would have left, but I felt like waiting. After the oldest boy got his haircut, the Arabian guy walked them back to their parents. The barber that cut the kids hair started talking about the boy's father.

Apparently, when the father first opened the store he wanted to put in gas pumps, but the bank wouldn't give him the money to do so. He flew back to Arabia and got the money from his people. That's how he got the gas pumps. I thought to myself, "No wonder he didn't like the banks."

I stepped outside to see the boys get in the truck with their mom. I noticed she went up Winchester. I walked back in to the barbershop to Greg fat ass saying, "Boy, I thought you was gone. I almost started on this big head joker." He laughed as he pushed some kid out his chair. I sat there getting my haircut in deep thought. I couldn't help but wonder where she was headed. I would have to no longer wonder.

We had the address. It was like having $10 in my pocket. It was cool. I knew where some money was at. I just had to figure out how to get it. I had her schedule down packed. It had to be her. That was the only way this would work. She would always go to Subway for lunch, then pick her children up from school. She would stay at the store for like an hour, then, her and her children would go home. She would usually get home between 8:00pm and 10:00pm. I noticed that 10:00pm was late for her.

I had borrowed a girl's dog I knew. I walked the dog through the neighborhood. I knew his wife so well. She turned the corner and hit the garage. She drove up the driveway into the garage it closed behind her. I continued walking the dog back to the Sonata. I put the dog in the car so that I could get a good idea about the property. As I rode pass I noticed a light came on. She was home. I kept driving back to the 'hood. I couldn't wait to tell Andrew what I had discovered.

I went to see Andrew the next day and told him everything I saw. He told me to wait until Daylight Savings Time because it would get dark early. I knew exactly where she would be, at the time I said she would be there.

Some nights I would wait up Winchester just to see what time she was going to pass by me. I knew exactly how long it took her to make it home. I didn't have any money. But I was paid in my mind. Terry got tired of me asking for 20 here 20 there. Hell, it got hard to get $10 out of him. It was getting close to my Birthday. Two weeks went by fast. This was considered a mission and it required being dropped off, so that you could already be in position once your victim arrived. The only way to complete the mission was escaping in the victim's car. That's why it was important to wait until Daylight Savings Time. That way no one would notice them waiting on her to arrive.

I dropped them off around 6:30pm. They had been in the yard at least a good hour and a half. I went back to the store to wait on her to leave. The first part of the mission was to let them know she was on the move. Once I paged them twice in a row, they would get ready because she would be close. Once I saw her and her children getting in the truck, I would page them with Andrew's partner's cellphone. Then, I would drive off.

I knew exactly how long it would take her to make it to River dale. Once she passed me on River dale, I paged them twice. I knew they were positioned in the yard waiting on her to pull up. Those were the longest 20 minutes of my life. Then, I saw her truck burning rubber coming through the light headed right past me. I knew they had the money. I jumped in behind her truck, followed it to the back of the Super K Mart store where I was already sitting, When we met up I opened the back door to the Sonata, while they were unloading the safe from her truck. It was big and looked heavy. I was hoping it would fit. They didn't hesitate in getting the safe out.

We left a bag of coins behind. I turned on River dale and headed for the expressway. Once I made it on 385, I drove 70 mph. Andrew and his partner were hype, but I knew I had to stay calm, so I didn't go over the speed limit.. I couldn't help but wonder about how much money we had took. A Sheriff's car coming past me broke my train of thought as it came by me with their lights on, but no siren.

Going back to where we just left. I kept mobbing and jumped off on Perkins. Stopped at the red light, looked to my left, and saw the police. He looked at me I looked at him then the light changed. We both started driving down the road. He turned off, I kept rolling. I had a anxious but calm feeling about what we had just done, basically i didn't give a fuck. The Sonata was a girl car no-one looked at it twice.

We pulled up to Andrew's partner's house and got the safe out the car. Andrew's partner offered us something to drink. I said, "A Coke" and gave him his cellphone back. It was time to get down to business, now.

We used a crowbar to pry the door hinges off the safe. I looked at them as I was sipping the Coke anxious to see what was inside. Once the safe was opened, I couldn't wait to find out how much was in there. The money was in stacks of $50,000. Five $10,000 stacks. This is how we divide it: $50,000 for you, $50,000 for you, $50,000 for me. $50,000 for you, $50,000 for you, 50,000 for me. We did this until I noticed I was looking at $450,000 dollars and there was still more money in the safe!

I looked at Andrew and said, "I told you it was more than $300,000." He kept pulling money out of the safe. He finally stopped. It was close to $600,000 in there. Split up three ways, we got to a $190,000 a piece. Andrew said he was cool with what he had. So, I got $7,500 more. I totaled out at $197,500. We threw the safe in the BFI garbage can, put our money in pillowcases and walked out the house looking like Santa Claus. Once I made it home, I walked in the house and put my money up. My sister was doing Melody's hair. I gave them $500 a piece and walked back out the door. Melody said, "Dog, how much money you win." I said. "A lot." I jumped back in the car and headed to the liquor store. Andrew grabbed a bottle of Don Perignon Extra Dry. We headed to his apartment. He grabbed his money and we walked to his door. He went in the room with his girlfriend. I could hear her scream with joy. I called Terry on Barbwood.

He came to the phone and said, "Hello." All I said was, "I'm rich."
He started talking shit.
I said, "Be cool. I'll meet you at the house in like two hours.
Andrew opened the door and I walked back there. His money was on the bed. His girlfriend was ecstatic. She went and got glasses for the Champagne. She prayed
for us before we took down this score and after. Then, I tasted the nastiest shit ever. Don Perignon. I couldn't see how people liked celebrating with this disgusting champagne. I said, "I'll stick to Moët."
Once Andrew put his money up, we jumped back in traffic. I met Terry and
Zo at the house and went to get my money to show it to them. As soon as
Zo saw it, he didn't won't no part of it. He kept saying it's too much money. "They're never going to stop looking for y'all.", he continued. Terry was too busy in shock. Hell, I think Zo was, too. I had just told Terry the day before to let me get $10. I also told him that after the robbery, I wouldn't need his money anymore. I knew that's what he was thinking about. I put my money back up. I told them I would come get them the next day.

Autobiography of Samuel Plain jr.

Andrew and I left I spent the night at his house. We got up early the next morning. I didn't sleep much. I was too busy thinking about all that money. I couldn't eat, either. We mobbed to the car lot to get something else to ride in. Andrew bought two cars. One for his mother and one for his girlfriend. I was sitting down counting my money when the car salesman asked me did I want a car. I told him I was cool. This shit took all day long and it was not how I planned on spending my day.

Once the paper work was done on his, cars we dropped off his mother new car in her driveway. I told Andrew I would get up with him later and headed to the house. I still hadn't eaten anything. I tried to eat but I only could take a few bites. This was unusual because I loved Jack Pirtle's chicken. Once I got home I took a short nap. Then Raegan called telling me that Destiny needed diapers. I jumped up to make sure it wasn't all a dream. This was really the only sleep I had in like two days. I stopped by Walgreens to get diapers then headed to Raegan's house. I stayed there the rest of the day. I got up around 3am that morning and went to the house. I stayed up thinking. I didn't go back to sleep. At 9am. I called this White gentleman that stayed around the corner from the house. His wife was selling her '94 Cadillac SLS. I walked to their house, and rang the doorbell.

He answered the door saying, "How's it going, Man?"

I said, "Cool. Remember me from the store?" "You remember I told you I was going to buy your wife's car?"

He said, "Yes, so you have the $17,500."

I said "Of course." He had this pleased look on his face like he was relieved.

He went on to tell me that the note on the car was kicking his ass.

I remember thinking, "So that's what that look meant." I gave him $10,000 to start with. This guy looked at every ghost in every bill. I sit there trying to be patient. He was looking at Ben Franklin and trying to find his ghost at the same time. Once he got to the last bill. He said this is only ten thousand. I said, "I know", and handed him the rest of the money. He looked for Ben's ghost in every last bill, again. Ben didn't disappoint him. He showed up in every last bill. Finally, he was finished. By then his wife had cooked me some breakfast. I couldn't help but to notice how pretty she was. Her sweet manner made her attractive. I ate everything on my plate; I was hungry.

I followed the couple to the bank in my new car. I was reluctant to let them hold my money. I was scared as fuck when I walked in the bank. I thought the police were going to jump out any moment now. The man gave the banker the money to send to a bank in Texas. The bank his wife had gotten the car loan through. The banker wrote out me a bill of sale for the car. She smiled and told me, "Congratulations." I said, "Thank you", and walked outside. I shook their hands and jumped in my new car and drove off. I have never been scared to spend a lot of money at one time since.

I picked up Terry in my new car. It looked just like the car that Sam had got for me in the Summer. I did that on purpose. That way I didn't pop up with no new shit. The only difference was this car was a 1994 and the car Sam got me was a 1995 plus this car had an ugly ass top on it. A tan cloth top. I hated it but it was a perfect excuse to why I hadn't been driving my car. Terry and I mobbed up to Cadillac of Memphis on Covington Pike. I spent $3,600 on some Fat Boys and Vogues. It took almost an hour. They were super-fast.

It was like 1:00pm that afternoon. I was hurting the town with my new creation. We went straight to Stereo One so I could get bumped out. This shit took all day. I called Andrew to come get us from the Stereo One where I left my car. I got two Amps crossed over with built-in cooling fans, three JL audio 12-inch subwoofers, two 6 x 9 Kenwood speakers, tweeters with the build in Mids, the Kenwood radio that came with CD and cassette player. The radio was $1200 by itself. In total, I spent like $3,300 on my system. I paid for everything and left.

Andrew was looking for a newspaper to see if we made the news. Lo and behold, it was front page! The Commercial Appeal read: WOMAN BEATEN; ROBBERS TAKE SAFE FROM HOME WITH $500,000. She told police that as she was taking a pan of spaghetti from the vehicle, two men who were crouched in the corner approached her and knocked her to the ground. They pulled out semi-automatic pistols. The men demanded money, forced the woman into her home and tied her hands with telephone cord. They then beat her head on the floor, demanding valuables. The suspect searched an upstairs bedroom where they found the safe and rolled it down the stairs. They drove away with the safe in the victim's 1996 GMC Jimmy. Police did not speculate as to why the family kept $500,000 in their home. One of the family's stores had been robbed of $50,000.

I was shook I didn't trust a soul after that. I had to keep everyone on the end of my gun from this point on. I remember thinking to myself I was now a fugitive from justice. Andrew started laughing talking about the store owners kids were like "who are you guys?" brought me out of this trance. He went on ,"She not lying, that safe was heavy as fuck. I had to kick it down the steps. Her punk-ass tried to throw hot spaghetti on me." This was the first time he had spoken on how he found the money and where he found it at. He went on to say that he looked in that room first, but didn't see anything so he shut the door back. After looking all over and still not locating it, he opened that door all the way up to see the safe sitting in that room by itself. The reason for the phone-cord is because they wanted her to be able to get free.

This money had changed me, I no longer felt safe. I knew people was looking for me high and low. I'm sure everyone wanted a piece of this money. I felt in danger.

"Is this what having a lot of money feels like?", I asked.

Andrew answered, "Yep. Don't worry it will grow on you."
We pulled back up to my car and it still wasn't done. Terry rolled a blunt up. I asked the guy working on my car could we smoke outside. He said sure they were closed anyway. My car was the last car of the day. I went back inside. I already knew what I was about to do to this car. It would have been a beautiful car if it just didn't have this top on there. "It had to go", is was what I was thinking. The dude working on my car interrupted my thoughts and motioned me over.

He showed me how to work my radio with a remote. I remember pulling my car out for the first time when it had Beat in it. Earlier that day, when I was waiting on Andrew to pull up, I had walked across the street to Pop Tunes to buy some CDs. I got Jay-Z's new CD. I was bumping It's a Hard Knock Life. The beat went hard and Jay went even harder. I never liked Jay Z. because Tupac didn't like him. But this guy was a solid cat. Let's stick up the whole world and split it 50/50. Now I was a fan of his music.

Things had started looking up for me again. I was the second owner of this car. It had 33,000 miles on it paid for and, I didn't have Sam coming at me with no Insurance bullshit. I didn't have no Insurance, but I had some "Just in case some bullshit happen" money.

I didn't have time to go to the Mall because Stereo One had taken so long. It was cool, as long as we caught the liquor store. We bought a case of Moët. It's always been my favorite Champagne. At 12:00am it would be my birthday. I would be turning 20yrs old. Andrew was right this money was growing on me. Hell I see why republicans don't give a fuck about the poor. Ive always been cocky, but this was the beginning of a arrogant little motherfucker. I didn't go in no clubs that night. We partied in traffic pouring champagne out dancing. Like we had just won the Super Bowl. Pouring champagne in girls mouths. Fire up blunts getting them drunk. Every club we hit we did some parking lot pimping.

We stayed in traffic all night. I checked in the Holiday Inn off Perkins with two girls I had met at the Mirage. I literally fell asleep inside one of the females. To my surprise I woke up in some pussy. I gave the girls cab fare once they were out the door. I took a shower, then I drove across the street to the Mall of Memphis to get fresh for my birthday.

I grabbed a Tommy Hilfiger outfit out of Dillard's and a fresh pair of Icy White Reeboks. I still was wearing Fahrenheit cologne. At this time, it was my absolute favorite fragrance. We hit D&D for my birthday. It was crunk ass fuck in there. I balled out all weekend. I didn't know how I got home but I was at the house in my waterbed. I had the worst fucking hangover. Ever since I had gotten that car I had been staying out the 'hood and hadn't been going home.

It was Monday. I had a lot to do this week. First thing on my list was to get my car painted and get this ugly ass top off it. I took it to Bobby Smith on Beale Street. Then Bobby and I went to see the twins at Don's Upholster. I told them that once the body work was done and the paint job was finished, I wanted a top the same color. I was painting it White Diamond and I wanted it trimmed in gold. They said it would take about a month, I said good.

Terry followed me up there in the Sonata. We jumped back in the Sonata after I paid up front for my car. Bobby charged me $2500 for the body work. That came with removing the old top and the paint job. Now that I got all the business with my car situated, it was time to remodel the house.

I spent the rest of the week picking out kitchen cabinets and tile for the floor. I put wall to wall carpet all through the house and new furniture. I even changed all the ceiling fans. This renovation would take a couple of months.

Two weeks had passed. I went to Bobby Smith to check on my car. He was done painting it. It was ready to go to Don's in the morning. I couldn't wait to get my car back. The house was a wreck, the floor was looking crazy. They had to tear the floor before laying the tile down. The carpet man had to pull the carpet up before laying new carpet down. It was so much shit on the street for the garbage man to pick up. Finally, the carpet man was done and my car would be ready later that day. Everything was going as planned and I would have my car and house exactly how I wanted them.

It had been a month since I dropped my car off. When I got to Don's it was just like I wanted it. Altogether, I spent $5,500. I was driving down the street and saw this guy's Cadillac. He had a piece of Chrome that went around the wheel base. I turned around and went back up to Don's. I asked Terry or Jerry, I always get them mixed up, to order me some.

He said, "No problem."

I said, "I want them gold, too" and gave him $600.

He said, "Give me time to get the parts in and dip them."

That was all I needed to hear.

I shut down traffic with my new creation. This girl I knew ran up on my car and knocked on my window. I almost shot this female in the head. She started screaming once she noticed I had that 357 pointed at her face.

I rolled down my window and asked, "What the fuck you want?" She said, "Why you always pulling guns on me?"

I asked her again, What do you want?"

Peaches said, "You acting funny."

"Naw.", I said. "You full shit. When I asked you to help me get my car out the shop you acted like $5,000 was too much for you to reach for. Now that you see me back shining you all on my dick."

I never took the gun off her.

She smiled because she knew I was right. Then that smile turned to a look of concern, when I pulled the hammer back on the revolver. I saw her head disappeared.

Traffic at the Mirage was thick. When I pulled up, I saw Peaches bullshit ass that worked at Ebony Lace. she ran me hot one night in the Sonata. When I first met her, I was in the Cadillac SLS. Then, I put it in the shop. When I started asking her to help me get my car, although I had already paid for it anyway to get out of the shop, she proudly declined. Now that this female saw me shining, she wanted to run up on me like we cool never. Everyone was digging my car. I was killing 'em.

Terry passed me the Hennessey. That's when we caught eyes. She was staring at me and I was staring back at her. She said, "Wassup?" She was cute. I said "Wassup sexy?" Pull down there and park, I'll pull up on y'all."

I told Terry to get down on her friend. We drove through traffic and parked. Terry fired the weed up. I saw her Black Rodeo sport pull up. A White girl jumped out, but it wasn't the girl hanging out the window. "Wait a minute.", I thought to myself, I know this female. This was same girl I tried to talk to on Beale back in the Summer and now she was trying to act like she was all that.

She walked up and said, "Wassup?"

I said, "Ain't shit up. Where your friend go?"

She was fine as fuck though, but I had to reject her. The only reason she was over there was because of my car now. It was no secret.

When her friend got out of the truck, I was impressed. She was cute and fine. What I thought was a redbone was a White girl that she was cool as fuck and was down to Earth. She walked up with a straight face at first.

Then she started to laugh once she leaned in my ear and said, "That bitch always do me like that. I'm so glad you turned her down you won my heart with that."

I said, "Well, let me call you.

She said, "You can call me tomorrow. We'll go do something, but tonight, I'm too drunk. I just got off work."

I said, "Where do you work?"
She said, "Platinum Plus."
I asked, "Awe, you dance?"
She said, "Yep" and kissed me on the cheek. She whispered in my ear,

"Call me."
I said, "What's your name?"
She told me her name was Gee and that her real name was Jennifer. I said, "I'm Samuel. Nice to meet you."

Terry was talking to her snooty friend Carmen. As the girls walked off I winked at Terry and said, "I got me one. Let's go." We left.

We got out of traffic. I had gotten chosen up on by a fine ass White girl that worked at Platinum. Her body was like a work of art. You wouldn't believe the best part about her, she liked me back. I went to the house and crashed out. I dreamed

about this girl that night. I got up around 2 that afternoon. I called Jennifer, she was still sleep. I could hear it in her voice.

I said, "Get up, nothing comes to a sleeper but a dream."

She said, "Shit, what time is it."
I said, "3 something."
She replied, "Let me jump in the shower and throw on some clothes." I said, "Hurry up, I'm waiting on you."

I gave her directions and she said that Carman knew where Knight Road Elementary was. I told her that the house was right in front of the school.

Jennifer and Carman pulled up to the house I was outside on the phone. Even though I meet her at club Mirage, and dreamt about her all night, let's just say I touched a dream. We hugged and I invited them in the house. I told them to excuse the mess because I was getting the house renovated. Carmen uppity ass had her fucking nose up talking shit. I told Gee let's go outside so we could talk.

Once outside I asked, "Wassup with your friend? She bout got roasted. She's lucky I like you."

She laughed and said, "I know. I'm going to call you later. Is that a cellphone?", she asked. That's the number you gave me?

I said, "Yep."

Everyone couldn't afford a cellphone back then. Hell, my phone bill was like

$700 to a $1,000 a month, depending on how much I talked on it. Gee said, "Let me shake her and I'll call you later." I looked to see this lil uppity walking outside. Gee said, "She's not feeling your friend." "It's cool", I said, because he was bout to cuss her out anyway. It was funny because we both knew our friends so well. We hugged again. She said, "See you later, handsome."

After they left Terry, told me he almost cussed that female out. I was laughing because I knew he was on the voyage of doing so. Gee hit me back like 30 minutes later and told me she was ready and stayed on the phone with me giving me directions. We went to O'Charley's on Winchester, ate, and had drinks. She told me she was single and had just gotten out of a relationship. She cared about the guy, but was ready to move on.

Once we were done eating she had invited me over to Carmen's mom's house where she was renting a room. She told me she was from Jackson, Tennessee and that she had only been in Memphis for two months working at Platinum Plus. She still smoked joints. She pulled out some papers and rolled 2 of them. I was high as fuck. She told me she wanted to try on an outfit for me because she wanted my opinion on how she looked in it. It was a red Catsuit with a Santa Claus hat. She put it on and said, "How do I look?" I told her, "Like someone had the wrong girl. They had my girl." She laughed.

She asked me, "Have you ever kissed a White girl before?" I told her, "No."
She said, "I love your lips. Can I kiss you"?
Of course I said, "No."
She did it anyway.
It was intoxicating. I had never dated outside of my Race. So, this kiss was
exciting and different. I was really feeling this girl, but I couldn't show it. See, women want what they can't have. The only thing was that she could have me alright but I couldn't show it. It's always a thrill to see a woman try to seduce you. Women hate rejection. Although I wasn't rejecting her, in no sense of the matter. I just was making her want me more.

We fired the other joint up. This girl was a movie star that hadn't been discovered yet. She asked if I would come see her once I got off work that night.

I asked her, "What time you get off work?"
She asked me, "What time was it?"
I looked at my phone and said, "9:03 pm."
She said, "Shit, I have to start getting ready for work. I'll be here by
3:30am I'm getting off at 3:00am. Are you going to be up?" I said, "Yeah, just call me."
I grabbed my gun and put it in my waistline.

She walked me to the door and asked, "Can I have another kiss, handsome?" This time I let her kiss me and told her, "I could get used to this."

I put one foot back in the door and she smiled and said I got to go to work crazy.

I shot around the corner to the Corner Pocket. It was on Perkins. The Corner Pocket was a pool hall that I would hang out in. It was like an oasis in the 'hood. I would gamble and play pool most of the night. The man that ran the pool hall was a pool shark. I knew he would buy crack with my money, but I didn't care. I was paying for pool lessons. That's the only way I can rationalize losing my money to him knowing he was buying crack with it. See to be the best you must sit at the feet of Masters, That's how you become great at anything in life. Plus, we were only playing $10 a game. That was something small to a giant.

The police walked in about 12:50 am. He knew the owner of the pool hall and had a key. As soon as he walked in the door, he said, "What is this game worth?" We said, "Only $10." He said, "Last game. Shut it down." Pops was supposed to be cleaning up by now. The officer rode past the pool hall and saw the lights on after 12 and knew that we were gambling. I was down like $70. I was killing time until Gee got off work, anyway.

I headed to Barbwood to holler at Terry and see what was going on. It was dry as fuck out here. There wasn't a soul in sight. I went in the house to find Terry smoking a blunt. He passed me the blunt and got up and went in the kitchen and came back with a big bowl of banana pudding, Mama Mabel had made."This weed good fool. It got me with the munchies.", he said. I had been drinking Coronas at the Corner Pocket. I was glad to be smoking some weed to level this buzz out.

Gee called at 3:20am to tell me she was at the house and to meet her there. I pulled up and rang the doorbell. She opened the door. She was wet she ran back and jumped right into the shower. I got a glimpse of her ass as she turned the corner. I went into her room took my shoes off and laid across the bed. She screamed from the shower, "Roll a joint." I screamed back, "I have a blunt." I had grabbed some weed from Terry. Plus, I didn't know how to roll joints. She got out of the shower with only a towel on and started lighting candles.

She asked, "Are you comfortable? Do you want anything to drink?"

I told her, "Yes, because this weed going to give me

cotton mouth." I asked her "What did y'all have?"

She asked Pepsi, orange juice, or water?"

I said, "A Pepsi would be fine."

I fired the blunt up. She returned with the Pepsi. She had a can and a glass in

her hand. She opened it and poured it. This girl knew how to cater to a man. She turned the lights off and laid right beside me.

I asked, "How was work tonight?"

She said, "It was cool. "I made like $480.

I passed her the blunt. I stared at her admiring her beauty as she took a drag

from the blunt.

She said, "Get comfortable. I'm not going to bite you." I said, "Yeah, right." as I started to get undressed.

She said she was cool on the weed. So, I put the blunt out. I was laying there only in my boxers when she started to rub my chest. This time, she didn't ask if she could kiss me, she just did it. I removed her towel. She removed my boxers. She got on top of me and inserted my manhood inside her. She rode my dick like it was her favorite position. We both was so into it that we didn't notice what happened next. I heard her say, "Oh shit! The fucking pillow is on fire!" She started swinging at my head putting the fire on the pillow out. I moved my head out of the way of her mighty blows.

She managed to put the pillow fire out but not the one in us. We laughed so fucking hard. This was the funniest shit in the world. I grabbed her and this time I took charge. I watched her eyes roll in the back of her head as I folded her up like a pretzel. Her submissiveness was turning me on beyond control. I would make sure her womb was sore before the morning was over. We fired the blunt up after we was done and started to talk.

I asked her, "What she wanted out of life?"

She said, "Everything."

I gave her a look of disbelief as I told her she could have everything she

thought she wanted with me. She had a curious look on her face. She said, "Why did you say it like that?"
I said, "Because you're going to get used to everything you thought you wanted."

She was different. She would rub me until I fell asleep. I woke up excited. Don's Upholstery called to tell me that my parts had made it in. They had already sent the parts off to get them dipped in gold. Gee told me to come back to bed. I didn't exchange words with her. I fell back to sleep and ended up sleeping all day.

We got up around 3:30pm that afternoon and went to Applebee's for lunch. I got some crazy stares from Black people and White people. This interracial dating would take some getting used to. Black girls looked at me like I was the scum of the earth. White men looked at me like they wanted to kill me. Gee was used to this. She would ask people, "What the fuck are you looking at?" If you have ever seen I dream of Jeannie, this was Gee. She was down with me like Jeannie was down with Major Nelson. Gee went Downtown with me to Don's to get the gold pieces put on my car. We became best friends. I took Destiny over there to meet Jennifer. She fell in love with her. Destiny had her mug on like always. Everyone thought this was so funny. Here you have a little girl with a mean mug on her face. People would be shocked that she knew how to do this. The funny part was this little girl was serious. Destiny had a very good Christmas. I took her to Toys "R"Us. She picked out all the Teletubbies. Gee got her so many Tommy Hilfiger outfits and shoes. New Year's was in a week.

THE WINTER of '99

Gee went home to Jackson, Tn. We hadn't talked in a week. She called me on the phone to tell me that she had moved back to Jackson and that she was going to give her old boyfriend a chance. She cried like a new born baby. I played it smooth and told her it was cool and to do what's best for her. She said, "I really do love you." I said, "Well, if it's meant to be, you will be with me." She got an apartment up there and had it furnished. I wished her the best and hung up the phone.

I was sitting there staring when my sister asked, "What are you thinking about? All you do is wait on that White girl to get off work. Then no one sees you for days." I replied "So, stay out my business." I learned then no matter how much money you have it can't make you happy. Then I said, "You're right, I'm sorry." My sister knew when something was bothering me. I had to get out the house and do something to keep my mind off Gee.

I was so close to getting up on Ralph. He owned the club Gee worked at. I knew this was my pay day. Gee was none the wiser about how I get my money. She had no idea that Ralph was on my hit list.

We all where at the Corner Pocket playing pool, When Zo got in to it with Lil Robert. He wasn't a threat, but for some reason, they treated him like he was. Robert was talking slick as hell until Zo hit him in his mouth. That's when Andrew

came across his head with a pool stick. He ran out the door screaming threats like "I'll be back. Y'all got me fucked up." Lil Robert was a hustling little motherfucker. He was from Mississippi. He used to buy deals from me. By no means was he a real threat. We left the Corner Pocket after the fight. I guess Andrew forgot he told Victoria to come by the house. Victoria was driving a car just like Lil Robert. For a minute, I thought it was his car, too. I grabbed the Single Shot 20-gauge.

Terry and Andrew stood at the end of the side walk. As the car turned the corner, they began to fire upon it at will. I could only hear the 357 Terry was shooting. I took aim at the moving car and fired once. The car kept going. I said, "Y'all tripping. That ain't dude car. Minutes later Victoria called and screaming, "I can't believe you shot me. You looked me right in the face and shot me." The only thing saved her life was a necklace she was wearing. And that he was carrying a 32 revolver. The Bullet hit the gold necklace then grazed her neck. This female was in love with him after that.

She danced in Memphis but had a house in New Orleans. Zo was on probation for that cocaine charge. He had a warrant for violation of probation. The Sheriff captured him three days after the accident with Lil Robert. We jumped on the road and went to New Orleans.

I never in my life been on a bridge that was so long that you needed pay phones on it in case you have car trouble. It seemed like the water was going to come on the bridge. I couldn't wait to get off this damn bridge. Victoria had a house full of young females that did everything she said. They danced in New Orleans, too. She introduced me to a cute girl name Cherry. Andrew was a player hater. The first thing he said when he saw Cherry was, "You know he only likes White girls, right." I was shocked. I tried to clean up him saying this bullshit. It did no good. The seed was planted.

I hadn't thought about Gee until he said that bullshit. Now, she was on my mind.

Cherry said, "So, you only date White girls huh?"
I said, "No I like all women."
She said, "Well I'm a hoe I sell pussy. Do you still like all women?" "Of course.", I replied.

Victoria had already put me up on game and I could tell this girl liked me before Andrew, said that playa hating ass that bullshit. It was almost like there was no coming back from that comment. Every time I said something, this female would bring up me liking White girls. I wasn't feeling her the same way. Cherry, was getting real money, though. It was time to see what else New Orleans had to offer. So, I had to go shopping. I needed to clear my head anyway.

I spent a bankroll shopping on Canal St. That Sunday we got on down and went back to Memphis. I missed Destiny, so, I went over to Raegan's to get her. I could tell she missed me too. She heard my beat in my car as I was pulling up. I saw her dragging her bag in one hand and her car seat in the other. She was jumping up and down at the door. I put her car seat in the car and strapped her in.

I was almost home when the police stopped me for no reason, as usual. He jumped out his car and asked for my driver license. I gave it to him and turned my

radio up. Destiny started back to dancing then this dick head comes back to the car upset saying, "You better turn this shit down in this baby ear. You're lucky your License are valid because if they weren't, I'd be taking your stupid ass to jail. What the hell wrong with you got that shit that loud in that baby hear." He was right and I knew it. But he also was a player hater. So, I didn't let his ass get away with calling me stupid. I said, with a smile on my face, "Fuck you!", and turned my music back up. I shitted on his authority and then I spanked off on him.

I was playing Peekaboo with Destiny when the phone started ringing. I answered the phone. It was Lucy, Gee's friend. She said, "Toot, this is Lucy."

I said, "Wassup."

Lucy said, "Oh nothing. I was calling to tell you that Gee wants to know if she can call you."

I said, "Why she didn't call?"

She said, "Good question. I don't know, Toot."

I said, "Yeah, tell her its cool."

The phone rang, again. It was Gee.

"Wassup?", she said.

"Shit, what you want to be up?" I replied

"I know you mad."

"Yeah, right. Just know I'm not a spare tire."

"I never meant for you to be. But you have to understand I felt sorry for

him. I've been giving him all my money. He had no money. His bills, everything, I paid for it. But I don't love him anymore. I love you, Toot."

"Get the fuck out of here!"

"No, seriously.", she said. "I want something out of life and I don't want to be in Jackson anymore."

I replied, "Look, if you're serious, move all that

furniture down here to Memphis and we'll get an apartment together."

"Are you for real?", she asked.

"If you leave him and bring everything to Memphis I have no choice because I'm telling you to leave your home."

"I can put everything in Connie's garage, until we find a place. I'm so excited. Let me get the phone book and start looking up moving companies."

I said, "I'll believe it when I see it." Then hung up the phone.

Andrew called and told me to come outside. I walked out the door to see he had gotten a '96 Chevy impala SS. This motherfucker was running. I told him to drive Destiny around the block so she could go to sleep. This always worked when I wanted to leave the house. When we pulled back up to the house, low and behold, their she was, a sleeping angel. I walked her in the house and gave her to Melody. I jumped back in the SS. This was a fast car stocked with no modifications. So, imagine if anywhere done how fast this car would be. My partner Q. had a Z-28. Q. had

been seeing us in traffic. He wanted to race Andrew. So, we met up on Sweeney Road. That Z-28 ran off and left that SS like it was standing still. Q. won $500 off Andrew. I got back to the house about 9:30pm Destiny was up now playing with Ahmad. He wasn't walking yet. This fat baby had no plans on walking. I stepped over the children playing on the floor and headed towards the restroom. I had to pee so bad it hurt.

A week went by, I hadn't heard from Gee. She called early that Saturday morning like 9 something.

"Toot, I'm here."

"You're where?"

"At Connie's. Get up, I miss you."

I woke Terry up and told him to ride with me. This dude here so hard to wake up. And then when you did get him woke, he always thought someone had finally got him. He was always doing wrong to somebody.

I pulled up at Connie's. Gee's brother was unloading the moving truck. I said, "You think you're slick talking about you missed me. Your ass wanted some help." She burst out laughing. I said to her, "That's why I brought Terry." Gee's brother's name was Jeffrey. This was my first time meeting him. We put everything in the garage and I told Gee I'll be back later. I knew Terry wanted something for helping me move. That's when he said, "Lucci, you owe me a steak." I said, laughing, "I gotcha." Terry always called me Lucci, because he knew Meyer Lasky, Jonh Dillinger, and Charles luciano were my favorite gangsters.

We went to Shoney's on American Way. I was in a good mood at breakfast. I was telling Terry how I was about to move out the house and get my own place with Gee. He was on some fat boy shit as usual. He wasn't saying shit. He was too busy eating stacks of pancakes. I was thinking, I knew why I was feeling excited. All this coffee I was drinking that's what it was. I dropped Terry off on Barbwood. Then went to get Jennifer. We cruised around 240 twice. She passed me the blunt back as we had a long talk about what was to come.

I met Andrew later that day Gee and I was still together. I told him I was getting an apartment. He wanted to show me what he did to his SS. He spent like $15,000 on it. He changed everything about the engine and exhaust. No one in their right mind would pull up on this beast. Jennifer and I found a two-bedroom apartment. The apartment complex was called the Landings Apartments. We had access to a tennis court, gym, and swimming pool all on the property. I got Vince to help me move Gee's furniture into the apartment. I brought a king-size bedroom set. I gave Gee money to buy plates, silverware, glasses, towels, soap, and everything else we needed. She knew I didn't need her money. She just wanted me to have it.

Every day she would go to work and come home and give

me her money. She had introduced me to Ralph in '98. He would let me in the club but wouldn't let me drink. I was only 20yrs old and you had to be 21yrs old to drink. Ralph liked my girlfriend, a lot. He drove a Red SL 500 Mercedes Benz. He was a very small man. Gee knew everyone who had real money in Memphis because they would hang out in Platinum Plus. I remember the first time I took Gee horseback riding. Shelby Farms had the most awesome horseback

riding trail. Jennifer and I would get high ass fuck, then ride horses. We would race them together then walk the horses and just talk. We played tennis almost every day. We stayed across the street from a sporting goods store. I bought tennis balls and a racquets. I would always work up a good sweat doing this.

On days I wasn't hanging out with Gee, I would be doing my homework on Ralph. I would watch Ralph from the Denny's across the street. He wasn't always at the club. But he always parked his car in the same spot. Right In front of the club. Ralph had so much money that the four or five million I was about to take wouldn't hurt him. He had that to give away. Ralph became rich from 1-800 numbers back in the 70sand 80s.

I would often asked Jennifer was Ralph at the club. She never knew why I was asking. He was a fast driver so following him was out of the question. Trust me, I tried. I would have to wait on my people to run the Tag number off the back of his SL 500. The Tag number came back to various addresses. But this address off Poplar seemed promising. We would know for sure once we made our move. He would have to be kidnapped that's the only way this would work.

We would have to impersonate the police, hit the lights, and pull him over. The kidnapping would have to take place right on 240. We would have to be fast so no one would notice him being arrested. Once he was handcuffed and in the van, the hard part would be over. One of us would have to jump in his car to get it off the side of the highway.

Terry and I was at the Corner Pocket. I was gambling with Lil George $50 a game. I was up about $500 on him. Terry was side betting with no money. He was gambling on ass and

George was losing. He was paying me and Terry. Terry had won like $200 off George. He was broke, but told me he had some money at home. He was betting and both of us was talking shit until finally he said, "Follow me on Barbwood. I'm done." I won $600 off him. Terry won $300. He was acting like he wasn't going to pay Terry. I didn't give a fuck, as long as he paid me. Terry was betting on ass and George wasn't slow he knew Terry didn't have no money. Terry wasn't a gambler and George knew it.

Once we got to George's house, he went inside and came back out with a bankroll. Pealed me off a 100-dollar bill. I dapped him up and said, "I appreciate it." He showed all his gold teeth and said, "Yeah, Toot, you not the only one got money." He had about 10,000 dollars in his hand.

Terry asked, "Hey Mane, where my money."

George said, "Terry, your black ass didn't have no money in the first place you lucky you got that $200 off me."

Terry was hot, now. He said, "Hey Mane, your bitch ass better give me my money."

George said, "Fuck you Terry. You were betting off ass anyway."

I told Terry, "Mane fuck that shit. Let's go."

Terry said, "Sissy ass boy, I'll get my money one way or another." I was hoping

Terry would leave this shit alone. He had beat the George out of $200 betting

on ass. So, I didn't know why would he be tripping. Terry finally got in the car. He was so mad.

Terry said, "Did you see that bankroll that that trick had? I should have taken it."

I said, "Fuck dude and that little ass money he got."

Terry said, "Naw fuck that, he's going to pay me.

I never knew how much bullshit this pool game was going to get me into. Terry was the one that had the problem with George, not me. He paid me. I would have had all the money if Terry wouldn't have gotten in my business in the first place.

Terry wouldn't let this shit go. Him and some dude went on Barbwood and tried to rob George. The shit went totally wrong. First of all, they knocked on the door instead of waiting for someone to come out so they could march them in the house. George, answered the door. Once he saw the mask, he ran to the back of the house and jumped out the window. They gained entry and grabbed his baby's mama. One of them grabbed the baby laying on the couch, put the gun to the baby's head and demanded the money. George's baby's mama was going crazy. She couldn't possibly think clear with a gun to her daughter's head. I guess she was moving too slow for them. One of them threw the baby against the wall. George ran across the street and called the police.

They didn't get the money. Terry told me he looked across the street and saw George on the phone and told his partner to hurry up. They ran out the house up the street. Terry said he couldn't breathe with the mask on so he took it off. George's brother Los was sitting in the car smoking a blunt the whole time. He saw everything. He saw Terry take his mask off. It didn't take long for a warrant to be issued. Terry had a warrant for aggravated home invasion. The police were looking for him high and low. He tried to talk to Los a couple of days after it happened. Los ran in the house and called the police.

I had order some 20-inch rims from Tire Shop of Memphis. I paid $4800 for them. It took a couple of days for them to make it to Memphis from California. They fit perfect. The only issue was that the rims would scrub if you hit a bump. Sunday came and I hit up D&D. We didn't go in, I was parking lot pimping. Then we jumped out in traffic. As soon as I left the club, the police jumped behind me. I gave the pistol to Terry to stash. I hit the gas like the police wasn't behind me. This gave Terry a chance to put the pistol up. The police hit the lights. I knew they were going to pull me over, anyway. I waited on them to catch up on the side of the road.

The White police officer asked, "Where is Terry, Samuel? I know you guys are thick as thieves." This dick head really thought his joke was hilarious.

I said, "I haven't seen him."

The Black officer asked, "How much you pay for those rims."

I proudly said, "They were $4800. He said, "You're crazy as fuck." He

was a real player hater.

See that's what these guys do. They weren't the cool guys in school, so they love to see what the cool guys are wearing, saying, and doing now. The White officer asked Terry for ID.

Terry said, "I don't have any. My name is Mario. I'm Terry's cousin."

The White police officer said, "Tell your fucking cousin to turn himself in. I heard about what they did to that baby. If I catch him it's not going to be pretty."

Terry said, "Yes sir.", in his slave voice.

I said, "Are we done, my woman waiting on me."

The Black officer said, "Sure thing. You guys have a nice day." I turned the music back up, Bling Bling every time I buy new ride Bling Bling.

I smashed off into the night thinking to myself, Damn that was close. They almost had Terry.

I dropped Terry off at the house and told him to stay out the street and that I would be back in the morning. I pulled up to Platinum Plus. Gee come out and got in the car. She went in her money bag and handed me the money. I gave her the blunt to fire up. She could tell I had a lot on my mind.

She said, "Toot, I want to do something fun

tomorrow."
I said, okay I'm game."
"That's 900 dollars I could have made more but I was ready to go."

We pulled up to the apartment. I got out with my gun in hand, like always. Once we were inside, Gee jumped straight in the shower. She got out and came into the living room and said, "Damn Toot, you didn't roll a blunt." I said, "Yes I did, fix me a glass of tea." I fired the weed up. She asked me, "Are you going to tell me what's going on?"

I said, "Shit. The police looking for Terry." She said, "For what?"
I replied, "A home invasion."
She said, "You weren't involved, right."

I said, "Never! The only thing I'm talking about taking around here is some pussy."

She laughed and said, "No you're not." and ran to the bedroom. I ran behind her and jumped on the bed.

I said, "You want me to take it, don't you?"

She smiled and said, "Nope, you can have it."
I woke up to Destiny's Child singing Can You Pay My Bills. I looked at the clock, it was almost 1:00pm I woke Gee up so we could make the most of the rest of the day.

She said, "You don't have to take me anywhere. Just buy me a Ferret."

I looked confused and asked, "A Ferret?! What the fuck are you going to do with a Ferret."

She said, "Please Toot, I've been wanting one."
I took Gee to a pet shop that sold them. She had to have one. She named it

Feebie. I didn't know if it was I boy or girl. She didn't keep it in a cage. She just let it

run around the apartment. Feebie would steal shit all the time. Things like keys, socks, panties. Anything that she wanted. Now that I had Gee occupied and satisfied with Feebie, I had to check up on Terry.

I took him some Debo's to eat. I got him a 20-piece

hot wing meal. This wasn't his first time being on the run. He knew he had to lay low or lay down. I started buying guns. I knew a war was coming. I bought an M-14. This was a powerful rifle that fires a 7.62 mm. This was an old ass gun. But it was in good condition. I also brought an SKS. It is a Soviet semi- automatic carbine chambered for the 7.62x39mm round. I told Vince to keep the guns at his house. Vince didn't have my guns but a 3 days when the Feds ran in his house. ATF Agents confiscated all the guns. At that point, Vince decided to cooperate with the Federal government.

Of course, I heard about what happened. But I didn't know of any place in Downtown Memphis named The Clifford Davis Building. It was the home of the FBI, TBI, ATF, CIA, and DEA. I had no idea this place existed.

I asked Vince, "What did they say to you."
He said, "Nothing, they just said they'll be in touch and that I would
 have a court date."
I asked him, "How did they know the guns where in your house? Who did
 you tell and did you say something about me?"
He kept saying, "I didn't tell anyone." I knew Vince wasn't telling the truth. I said, "Mane, I feel like you lied when you said you didn't tell no one about them guns. How else would the ATF know they were in your house?"

He came clean and told me he had showed them to this cat name Tony Bovan. I asked Vince, "Where this dude at?"
He said he didn't want any more problems and that the FEDs just left. "I don't need no more trouble.", he told me.

I told, "Him you'll be straight."
I was thinking that I should keep this motherfucker close to me so I could get to the
 bottom of this. I wish I had done the very opposite.
Terry and I was waiting on the Roy Jones Jr. Fight to come on. He was still on

the run for that Home Invasion charge. I called Vince to tell him to take my sister to the laundry mat to dry some clothes. The dryer wasn't working. It stopped working that morning. Vince put all the clothes in the bed of the truck. I was waiting on big Reggie to bring me some popcorn weed. Everyone called it popcorn because it was in little balls. Big Reggie pulled up and served me 14 grams. Terry rolled a blunt. We couldn't wait for the fight to start. I heard a car pull up outside. It was Vince, my sister, and her baby. So, I sat back down. Then, Vince asked me if we were having a party. I said, "Party?!" That's when it hit me. The damn Police!

I heard the officer say, "Get on the floor now!" The baby was crying. My sister was screaming, "Don't hurt my baby!" That's when I saw a 12-gauge shotgun with a flashlight on the barrel of it. The officer said, "OCU, get on the fucking ground now!"

I laid down slowly. I didn't want this shotgun to cut me in two. Terry was a little reluctant to stretch his arms all the way out because that 4-inch barrel 357 with the pistol grip was under the couch he was sitting on. The police kept telling him to stretch out. He kept pulling his hand away from that gun. The officer said, "If you don't stretch out, I'm going to kill you." Terry put his hand under the couch anyway.

The officers handcuffed us and pulled us to our feet. The older officer asked, "What is your name? And say, "Yes Sir" and "No

Sir" before you answer me."

He asked if I was a Black Male and 166 pounds and if my name was

Samuel Plain, Jr.

I said, "Yes Sir. Hold on Sir, I don't have 166 pounds. Someone lied to you, Sir. He said, "You think you a smart ass don't you."

I said, "No Sir."

This police officer was no joke. I got saved when the other officer flipped over the couch and saw that 357-

revolver sitting in the exact spot Terry kept playing chicken with. He slapped Terry so hard, everyone in the house felt it. The officer said, "Is this what you kept reaching for?" Terry's eyes were so big trying to explain that's why he wouldn't stretch out. They searched the whole house. All they found was a two- ounce cooking tube and four rocks in a cigarette box. They asked me if I had any large sums of money in the house. I told them that I did because me and my girlfriend were saving to buy a house. They were so close to finding my money in the attic. They literally walked right over a $135,000 that day.

I had to throw them off the trail. So, I told them where I had $5,000 laying around. I heard an officer say "Bingo." He had found something. He had found the cigarette pack with the rocks. This was no doubt Vince's shit. He was the only person that smoked Kool cigarettes, but he fucking denied everything. I later learned that they had a warrant for the house, Gee's apartment, and my car. Terry and I started yelling at Vince telling him to take his charge, but it did no good.

They took me to my apartment. Gee was at home when they searched the apartment. One of the Officers teased me about Gee giving him a lap dance on the coffee table in her underwear. The police always had jokes. They didn't find anything so they were satisfied. The one Officer with the rubber band on his beard asked me, "Why are you messing up Jennifer's life?" I smiled and said, "You would think that."

They took us to their headquarters on Madison. My sister told Vince he was wrong and that he better tell those people the truth. So, he tried to turn himself in, but it was too late. By that time, the ink had already hit the paper. There was nothing that could change at this point. Once they told me I only had $3400, I understood why they were typing so fast. They had stolen my money. These police officers were with the shit. They had stolen $1,600 from me. I never did get any of the money back.

They took us to 201 Poplar. The jailhouse was so overcrowded that we had to sleep on the floor. I had to stay down there two days. Terry was under investigation for 72 hours for that Home Invasion charge Los gave him. My bond was $500. Terry
 bond was also $500 on the charges we had together. They found fingers prints on Terry's gun that came back to him. I hadn't sold any crack in a long time. I didn't have to. So, my fingerprints weren't on the two-ounce tube because I hadn't been cooking. They still gave me all those charges, though.
I believe they kept the gun because we never got charged with it. They knew who crack it was and still charged us after Vince turned himself in. See, Vince was working for the Federal Government. He was the one that got the house busted, Terry captured, and me arrested. He put those four rocks there before he took my sister to the laundry mat.

I got out of jail and my sister picked me up from the Exxon across the street. I asked her how did that crack get in the house. She said, "He didn't want to ride it around with them, so, she told him to put it in the drawer. I told her, "I never lay around drugs because you never know when the police are coming." She said, "He said he's going to go to court with you." So now I felt more obligated to keep this sissy ass boy close. I talked to my sister for like an hour then, I went home.

Gee wouldn't stop calling the house phone. I called her when I got to the gate because the police let me give her my wallet before they took me to jail. There was a White card you scanned before entering the apartment complex. Gee ran to the gate. She was so excited. I got my gun out my stash spot. The police always miss my gun. I jumped out, gun in hand and walked Gee back in the house. Once inside she jumped into my arms. I said, "Damn, I only been gone two days." She said, "Shut up." Then, she kissed me.

I jumped in the shower. I couldn't help but think

about Terry and jail. I wasn't happy at all. I hated to leave Terry in jail like that. I told Gee what the police said about her dancing for them. She laughed. I also told her about what the other police officer said about me messing up her life. She said, "Fuck him with his dumb ass beard." We both started laughing. Terry got out two days later the charges had been dropped. He was so happy when I picked him up. He fired the blunt up and asked me where Vince bitch ass was at. I told him be cool we still need him to take his charge. Terry said, "Fuck that. He should have taken his charge in the first place. I hadn't been on Barbwood in a few weeks. See at the begin of summer Marie, and one of her friends was smoking in the back room. She accidentally, burned the house down. Ms. Mabel had to move out her home. She paid cash for her house on Barbwood. From the money she had got from the airport when she sold her house on Durby st. The fire was so hot it melted blinds on Sam windows. His windshield wipers were melted on his car also. That night when Terry took his mash off Los saw them run threw Ms. Mabel old yard. That confirm it was Terry that ran in George house.

When Terry got out, he couldn't wait to go down there. I took him down there and I wasn't thinking about George or Los at the time. Shit, they had called the police to start with, so, I figured the shit was over with. All these they were doing was buying time to get strapped up. I pulled up thinking I was just going in the house. Once inside, I saw they were gambling. So, I jumped in the crap game. Everyone was happy to see Terry. They heard about what happened. I didn't feel comfortable without my gun. I had left it in the car because the last time Terry was on Barbwood, they called the police. I left my gun in my stash spot. I walked outside. That's when I saw George across the street from my car with his hands behind his back. I kept walking to my car. Then, Terry came out of the house and Lil Gary was behind him.

George said, "Y'all can't come around here no more."

I asked him, "Who the fuck you think you talking to?"
He said, "Mane you heard me, y'all can't come around here no more."
That's when I saw Los rack a round in his cyber.
"Y'all better get the fuck away from here, right now.", he said I told George, "Shoot your pistol MR." Then, got in my car.

I told Terry and Gary to get in the car. As I was driving off I saw Los shooting in the air. I drove to the house and parked my car. I told my sister to let me see the Sonata's keys. Terry grabbed the AK-47. It shot the same round as an SKS, 7.62x39mm, with a 30-round clip. I had my 9mm on me. We shot back down on Barbwood. Not ten mins later, I parked on Chuck and we jumped gates until we were right across the street from the house where the home invasion took place.

We waited in the dark for someone to come out the house. George walked out the house. Terry started shooting. George hit the ground. It looked like he was hit! We creeped back through the backyard to the Sonata. No one saw us come or go. The very next night I kept applying pressure. I parked on Wooddale and mobbed on Barbwood through the cut. Once we got up close to the house, we shot the house up. We started at the floor to make sure we didn't miss this time.

About a week later I was in the yard when I saw Jay. Jay was cool he used to buy deals from me. He had come by the house with George in the car on some bullshit while I was gone. I heard this guy came to my house looking for me. It was crazy because now everyone was involving themselves in this bullshit. As soon as I saw Jay, I unloaded my 45. Later that day he came back through. He got off two shots before. Terry started to fire back as Gary jumped and rolled on the ground as he fired back I took cover behind Terry. I thought Gary had got hit. He jumped on the ground soon as I heard the first shot. Terry was on top of his game that day. Lil Jay came back trying to murder somebody. I stayed the night at the house.

Gee called all the next day. She was mad that I didn't come home. I kept telling her I was coming. I was tired. I didn't get much sleep. I told Terry to hold it down and that I would be back. That's when I told him we had to stay together because a lot of people want us dead.
When I got home, Gee had already left for work. It was just Feebie and me. I was asleep until the phone woke me up. It was my sister. I could tell something bad had happened by the tone of her voice.

"Terry has been shot in the arm.", she said a little nervous.

"Where did it happen at?", I asked.

"Down street somewhere. He just left in the ambulance. I can see the

police retrace his steps from the blood drops.", she said.

I said, "Okay.", and jumped up and shot to the house.

I called Lil Gary and told him to meet me at the house. They had moved off Barbwood on Perkins so he was around the corner. When I pulled up, I saw Gary standing in the driveway with his pistol out. I walked in the house and saw the 45 sitting on the mantelpiece. There was blood on it. I picked it up and dropped the clip.

There was still one in the chamber. I said, "Damn, them dudes must have hit Terry with a chopper." I knew this because he hadn't fired one shot back. He called me on my cell phone and told me he would holler at me when he got out of surgery. I asked him if he was straight. He said, "Yeah who ever shot him had a chopper." I told him I knew it because he didn't shoot back. Terry told me he thought Jermaine shot him. He couldn't talk much longer because the doctor was coming in and he had to go into surgery.

I went to the hospital to see Terry the next day. He had a cast on his arm. Terry told me that the doctors had put a rod in his arm. He said the bullet had shattered his bone. I reassured him I would take care of it. I knew it wouldn't be long before I got a chance to count me one.

I caught Jermaine and his girlfriend going into Piggly Wiggly. Vince and I was sitting in the car waiting on them to come out the store. They got in the car and started to drive off. I follow them down Perkins. They turned right on Chuck. I rode up beside them and opened fire. I gave him five shots and his girlfriend five shots. Before my gun had jammed. He let go of the wheel and the car came over on to the Sonata. Once I hit the gas, the cars came apart. This Weak ass boy fired one shot. POP! I said, "They shooting back!" Vince said, "No, that was me." I turned right on Knight Road. The car Jermaine was driving just coasted through the stop sign real slow. I hated this gun made by Ruger P89- 9 mm. This gun always jammed up on me. I was in the front yard when Jermaine rode pass the house on the passenger side. He changed seats at the Piggly Wiggly. He had his girlfriend driving pass the house, but I spotted him. I rode pass the house and threw the gun out the window to Terry, I gave him a look to let him know that I had taken care of that.

I kept driving. I parked the Sonata at a friend's house. I put it in the shop that very next day. The car that came over on it messed the front passenger door up. The Sonata needed body work and painting. It would end up costing me $1500.

I kept applying pressure. Gary and I laid in yard for hours waiting on George to show up. I told Gary, "Hes not coming." As soon as we got in the car, he pulled up on Barbwood. This dude I had driving for me was nervous. He had never been put in a situation like this before. No one on Barbwood didn't know his car. That's why it was cool for the car to sit and wait on us. Soon as we hopped in the car, that's when George pulled up. I told my partner to drive real slow and to stop the car as soon as we get in front of this George. He did the direct opposite. He drove slow until he started hearing Gary gun go off behind him. George jumped on the ground trying to get under the car. I couldn't get a clear shot because this dude hit the fucking gas. I saw the glass jumping out the car. I wanted so bad to stand over him and finish this shit. For some reason, he started to go faster. Gary said, "I got him! Don't worry! I got that bitch!"

Pickwick, Tennessee is a small boating town that sits on the border of three states: Alabama, Tennessee, and Mississippi. Pickwick Dam holds water from the Tennessee River. We stayed on the camping grounds in a log cabin. Gee and I rented jet skis. The waves on the Tennessee River are so strong it could throw you off at any time. I was so distracted back in Memphis. I couldn't focus on what was important: Ralph. I let these suckers pull me in to some bullshit that had nothing to do with me. Once i got back to Memphis, I stayed out the way for the most part. Gee and I took Destiny to the Mid-South Fair. My Cadillac was so noticeable I couldn't go anywhere in Memphis. I guess George saw my car parked on Airways in front of the Mid south fair. Because soon as i turned on Lamar i saw him lagging behind me. Once i pass Lamar circle i started bucking at them instantly. Gee cover the baby up as they return fire. We got into a shoot out on Lamar. I save three shots in case i ran back into them before I made it back to east Memphis. See this beef was on site. Where ever we saw each other it was going down. I couldn't believe this weak ass dude tried me with my baby and Gee in the car. Gary was standing in the front yard when I pulled up. Gary was furious about what happened earlier. I took Destiny to Raegan and Gee to the apartment.

Gary and Terry had a move up they were about to put down. They would get up early in the morning and watch the Chinese man open the barbecue place. They would always take the clock off the wall because they didn't own a watch. He carried a briefcase in the barbecue place, every day. He cashed checks. Terry spent a lot of time with his girlfriend Joice. They would stay at different hotels in East Memphis. Gee and I found a three-bedroom two-bathroom house with a two-car garage in the Brandywine Community off Ross Road. Our apartment was right down street off Ross and Winchester. I brought all new furniture for the house. I brought a pool table to match my furniture. We had 'His and Her' sinks and a Jacuzzi tub. This was a beautiful home with a community pool.

Once we were settled in the house, Terry, Gary, and I would plan the robbery's and smoke weed all day. Lil Gary went home and fell to sleep. The police got him early in morning for warrant he had. I told him not to go home and that he was cool at my house. It was just me and Terry then. This is when I started to get careless. Gary Lil bother Cliff started to come over to the house a lot hanging out. Cliff was a good boy. He did everything his mama told him to do. Terry was begging me to bust this move with him. I had big fish to fry and I wasn't about to tell no one about Ralph. I got tired of Terry asking me to go with him. See, him and Gary were supposed to be doing this but he got locked up. I was like, "Fuck it." I knew this shit couldn't be worth no more than $10,000 and that's if we were lucky.

I parked my car on Perkins in front of Gary's house and jumped in a Grand Marquis I had brought just to do dirt out of. I parked behind the restaurant and Terry hide behind the BFI garbage can. The Chinese man drove a Black BMW. I saw the lights

on his car turn in. I saw Terry get into position. The man got out the car, to his surprise there was Terry looking at him like a monster. I pulled up looking like monster number two. Terry let off a shot and told the man to run in the other direction. He grabbed the briefcase and jumped in the car. We pulled off, turned right on Knight road, then a right on Chuck, then left on Perkins. We threw the briefcase in my back seat.

I followed Terry to drop off the Grand Marquis back at my apartment. Terry jumped in the car with me. We headed to the new house to cut up the money. It was only 5500 dollars in the briefcase. I was disappointed as fuck.

Terry was happy go lucky about this move because him and Gary's homework had paid off. Terry wasn't having any money at this time. He been on the run for a min now. Gary called home from jail I told him I had been fucking with Cliff.

He said, "Toot if you haven't never listened to me in your life listen now. My little brother will tell on you in a heartbeat. Don't be fucking with him."

I said, "I ain't doing shit with Cliff."
I was at the house washing my car when Cliff walked up.
I said, "What the fuck do you want?"
He said, "Mane, where you been? Them dudes tried to start some shit
   with me yesterday."
I asked, "Who?"

He answered, "Them guys on Barbwood."
"So, what you telling me for? Why you didn't take care of your business?" "I don't have a gun. Give me a gun. I bet I'll blow one of them suckers ass
   off."
"Yeah, right.", I said. "You not going to do nothing you to soft. Gary
   already told me don't be fucking with you like that. So, I'm not giving you a gun."

"I know how to make a bomb."
"Get the fuck out of here. You don't know how to make a bomb."
"All you got to do is buy the stuff I need."
"Okay...", I said in disbelief. "I'll buy it. How much it cost to make?" "Less than $50.", he said. "My teacher taught us how to make one." Now i knew better than to be going in a gun store to buy anything. This is when i got super careless and the feds started watching me.

I went in Guns and Ammo. I bought some fuses and black gun powder.
He said, "I need some PVC pipe."
"For what?"
"To put the gun powder in and drill a hole in the top so

we can put the
　　fuse in it.

I took him to get all the material. I didn't give a shit. I wasn't throwing no bomb nowhere. Hell, I didn't even think this shit would work. I was a Cowboy not Timothy McVeigh. He made it, just like he said. He took a nail and hit it with a hammer to puncture a hole in the top of the PVC pipe that he had put the gun powder and bullets in. Then he glued the caps on both ends of it. I told Terry to drop him and his bomb off at home. Cliff told me he would throw it later in the week.

He called me so he could come get the Grand Marquis to drive. I got Terry to drop him off at the apartments. I stayed in the bed with Gee. I didn't leave the house that night. He called my phone early in the morning talking about, "I did it! I did it!" I said, "You ain't did shit get the fuck off my phone.", Then, I hung up.

The next morning, I got up and when to the house. My sister asked, "Did you hear what happened? Somebody threw a bomb in that house where them boys be at that shot Terry." She said, "Sam told me this morning. I saw him at the store." "He asked me about you. I called Sam and asked him what happened. He said, "Mane it sounded like a bomb to me. I'm not for sure, though." I said, "Hell naw! No way!" He said, "Yeah, a bomb." I had to go.

I rode down Chuck. All I saw was what looked like the fire department. That's All. The ATF didn't put this on the news because that would've interfered with their investigation. It rained all that day. I couldn't wait for school to be out so I could find out what really happened.

I went by Gary and Cliff's mama's house. Miss Clara Mae answered the door and said "Cliff not here, Toot." "Did you hear about what happened this morning on Barbwood." I was shaking my head side to side. She said, "Two people got killed this morning. They say it was a bomb." I was looking at her like, You don't even know your son did this. I had to find Cliff! The whole fucking day went by. It was 9:00pm at night before I heard from him. He didn't tell me he had gotten a job at Kroger's. I went to pick him up and he jumped in the car talking about what he had done. When I made it back to the new house, Terry told me we should kill his little ass right now. I laughed and told him to tell Terry what he had did. Cliff said that he lit the fuse on the bomb and threw it inside the house.

I said, "Your mother said two people were dead."
He said, "Those are not the only people I done killed."

Terry said, "See, that's what I'm talking about. This little bitch will tell something."

I told him, "Hey, you don't have to lie to kick it. I know you not build like that, Cliff, so stop the lies. I hope you got sense enough not to tell anyone what you did."

My sister didn't feel safe at all after that and since she didn't know who threw the bomb in the house, she felt like she needed some protection. I knew she needed some, too. We just had to figure out what to get her. She told me she wanted a gun that she wouldn't have to reload. So, I went with her to the gun shop she bought her a Bushmaster M-16 that shot 223 rounds with a 30-round clip and a scope. Just in case someone tried to harm them when I wasn't around. The court ordered her to Jury Duty. She told me before she left for that week that a white man came by the house

walking a dog. She said he kept looking at the house real hard. She said, "I'm telling you. they watching you."

The next day I went by the house to check on Melody. I was outside washing my car when Cliff walked up to me. I saw the house I bombed. I wanted to see what had happened to that house so bad. They say 'curiosity killed the cat.' I rode down on Barbwood and soon as I hit the street, I got this weird feeling in my stomach. I rode pass the house looking to see what damage had been done by the bomb. That's when I saw Los running towards my car. The radio was so load I couldn't hear the shots but, I saw guys running and shooting at us. So, I laid down in my seat and hit the gas. I stopped at the STOP sign and rolled the window down and returned fire until my clip was empty. I smashed off down Wooddale and turned right on Knight Road. I pulled over to look at my car. I was doing good staying out the 'hood now this bitch ass boy had shot up my car. I couldn't let them get away with this. Terry saw us pulled over and jumped out with his gun in hand. He said, "What happened? I can see it in your face." I show him the bullet hole in the back door. I parked my car in my garage. I had Gee to rent me a car a 1999 Dodge Plymouth.

The next day I had parked the Plymouth on the street in front of my neighbor's house. This was a mistake. Her husband Tom had been stalking her all summer long because they split up. So, she didn't know whose car was in front of her house. She called the police. Officer Rick Butler pulled up and made me get out of the car and sit on the curb. He found the ski mask and gloves in the car. He said, "If one of my officers catch one of those rounds you guys been shooting around here, I'm going to come to this house and kill everyone inside. A good friend of mines was killed today. Officer Don Overton. I'm pissed the fuck off so don't give me a reason." This is what stopped me from retaliating that night.

I saw my cousin Ralph later that week. He was telling me to come to his party. He was going to get this shit squashed.

He said, "Lil Cuz, you a player what you doing carrying a gun."

I told him, "It's been going down all summer."
He gave me tickets to the party. Ralph asked me how many people was I

bringing. He gave me four tickets. The party was Saturday.
Terry and my court date was on a Thursday. Mark A. Mesler was our Attorney. I

was wearing a brown Zenati suit. I saw the two officers that had fucked up the Roy Jones fight and stole my money. Vince was there to take his charge. Gee looked amazing in her dress. We all walked into the court room. The Judge told one officer to wait outside while the officer with the rubber bands on his beard testified. The police officer said he found the rocks in a man sock draw. He was sure of it. Mark said he didn't have any questions for him. Then the Black officer came in the court room. He testified that the rocks were found in a baby's drawer with baby clothes. Mark asked the officer was he sure that he found it in a baby's drawer. The police officer said yes, he was sure of it because there was baby clothes in the drawer. Mark asked the Judge to dismiss the case

and she did. But the weed charge was going upstairs. I was happy that shit was over with.

I picked Corry up the next day, that Friday. I went to Guns and Ammo to buy black powder. I was going personally to make sure this shit went as planned. Corry had nothing to do with this bullshit I got dragged off into. When Terry and me pull that move I gave a guy 2500 for 750 Yamaha. I was riding my bike when Gee called me on my cell phone. Gee said, "Toot there's been a lot over Undercover cars riding through here." I said "Y'all tripping. I beat a case yesterday. Why would they let me walk? I'm straight. Ain't no one watching me." When I got home, Gee had cooked some tacos. Corry and I ate. Then, Cliff came over and we went in to the garage. I made the bomb this time. It was so easy. Corry didn't ask what we were doing. He stayed in the house. Once Cliff and I was done we went back inside.

Vince called me and asked me what I had going on. I told him what was up and told him what time I was leaving the house. I said we were pulling out around five in the morning. Gee told me not to leave the house. She said, "Let Corry drop Cliff off. Don't go." I said, "I'll be back." I didn't know that I wouldn't see the streets for a long time after that.

I started getting ready. I woke Corry up so I could take him home. I told Cliff to put the bomb in the car. While my sister was on jury duty, I grabbed her gun from the house. She didn't know I had it. It's funny because, later on, the head ATF agent, Michael Rolling, said that my sister had made a straw purchase for me. That shit didn't make any sense. I was 18 yrs old and I could have brought my own long gun. She got that gun for protection.

Once I let the garage up and backed out the driveway, I turned my lights on and started to drive up the street. I saw a lot of activity for this time of morning. Once I turned on Ross, there was a van coming down the street and a police car on both sides of the street. As I was sitting waiting for the light to change, I saw another van pull behind the car that was behind a van. That's when the police at the Red light blocked us in. He jumped out with his gun in his left-hand yelling, "Get your hands up right now or I'll shoot you dead." I told everyone to take their charges. That I would make their bond as I put my hands out the window. Then, the van pulled up and agents started to jump out. One of them fired warning shots. They pulled me from the car and laid me in the street. They pulled Cliff out the car. He had grabbed my gun off the fireplace and put it in his pocket. I heard them saying, He has a gun in his pocket.

The ATF agent asked me did I want to talk to him first before anyone else. I said, "No." He said, "Suit yourself." I heard one of the officers say, "Y'all about to get a basketball score." Then shut the door in my face.

It was daylight. They blocked off traffic in every direction. They put Corry in the car with me and drove us up the street. The officer that was taking us to jail let us watch the show. A robot came out of the bomb squad van. They sent the robot down the street to the rental car. I watched ATF blow this car up with a bomb I built. People started coming outside after the bomb went off. That's when the police took Corry and me to 201 Poplar.

On Oct. 17,1999, The Commercial Appeal read: BOMB Exploded AFTER POLICE PULL OVER, ARREST 3 MEN. A homemade pipe bomb exploded in a rental car in Hickory Hill Saturday morning after police had pulled the vehicle over and taken three suspects into custody. Authorities had received information that the subjects were in the possession of explosives and could be planning an attack, according to a police report. The police bomb squad was attempting to defuse the bomb remotely when it went off, causing "fairly significant" damage to the vehicle, said Todd Reichert, an agent with the U.S. Bureau of Alcohol, Tobacco and Firearms. No one was hurt in the explosion. It did detonate, and that is the problem you have when you have homemade bombs. Reichert said. "You don't know how they are designed to detonate, and that's what makes them extremely dangerous."

On Oct. 19,1999 The Commercial Appeal read: 3 FACE CHARGES AFTER EXPLOSIVE VIOLENCE An apparent feud exploded- literally-into a series of incidents, one of which resulted in federal charges against three people Monday. Federal agents and Memphis police detectives Monday were trying to unravel a string of apparent related assaults in the Hickory Hill neighborhood. The latest was an explosion of a huge, homemade pipe bomb in a rental car stopped by police on Saturday. The bomb authorities say, was intended to be detonated at 3404 Barbwood. Two men, Samuel Plain 21, and Corry Hurt 23, were charged in federal court Monday with possessing an illegal explosive device, and a 17-year-old, a student at Sheffield High, was in Juvenile Court custody in connection with the incident. The two adults will be held in Federal Correctional Institution pending a detention hearing Thursday. The three were inside the 1999 Plymouth Breeze rental car pulled over by Memphis Police and Bureau of Alcohol Tobacco & Firearms agents just before 5a.m. Saturday at Raines and Ross after a tipster said guns and bombs could be found inside. Authorities found four weapons including an assault rifle and three pistols in the car. And on the back seat, lying in full view, they found a 12-inch-by-4inch homemade black powder pipe bomb.

According to police reports, the three were on their way to 3404 Barbwood, the scene of a small explosion set off several weeks ago and at least one shooting incident. It was the largest (pipe bomb) I've ever seen ", said ATF resident agent in charge, Gene Marquez. Authorities would not say whether the intended bombing was gang related or whether others are expected to be arrested. The bomb was " juvenile and simple in make-up ," said Memphis Police Maj. Larry Godwin, "and highly dangerous." Black powder is " always unstable," and could have exploded at any time inside the car, he said. Police were unable to disarm the bomb, and instead minimized the explosion when they set it off inside the car. The explosion damaged the car extensively. But, they said, it likely would have done massive damage to 3404 Barbwood. A pipe bomb went off on the porch of the home on Oct. 8. No one was

injured, and less than $500 in damages was done. That was reported by Harvey Freeman or anyone at the home Monday night were unsuccessful. A witness told police that she heard the explosion and several gunshots, and saw a man running away from the Barbwood address, according to police reports. Police said at the time that bombing may have been in retaliation for a shooting that happened in the area several weeks earlier.

On Sept. 12, two residents of the house were followed by another vehicle, which came alongside them with its occupants shooting. Their car was struck eight times. One of the people inside the car shot at, according to the report, Jermaine Briggs, was charged with an

aggravated assault in which another man was shot. On Aug. 27, a man was walking in 3400 block of Barbwood when he was shot in the arm by man carrying an assault rifle. He said he saw two men then run into the house at 3404 Barbwood. Police would not comment on the possibility that the several incidents were related.

Autobiography of Samuel Plain Jr.

THE END

Made in the USA
Lexington, KY
02 April 2018